Preface

What is it that spurs a person to put pen to paper and document their life from as far back as they can remember?

In my case it wasn't nostalgia, I'm not that sentimental, it was more like dementia, not that I have it yet, but it is a family heirloom I have a good chance of inheriting one day, my mam being the last person in the family to receive it.

Spending the afternoon sorting through all her photos when my brother and sister and I were emptying her house and wondering who half of the characters captured within them were, well, it was quite the eye opener I can tell you. And it made me think, when my kids cart me off to the retirement home or the big retirement home in the sky, will either of them really know anything about the family I was born into? Will my collection of photos of the good friends I made when I was younger and the family members who have changed so much they bear no resemblance to who they are today, be just as puzzling to them as my mam's friends and family had been to me? Names from my childhood so familiar and beloved to me, wouldn't really have any meaning to my children and all the family legends that I hold in my heart, and there were so many of them, well, they would all be gone forever.

So with all that in mind, I've set out and started to do some good old fashioned research, okay, it may only be chatting on the phone with my sister and brother and making notes of instances from my childhood when reminders bring stories back to me, but I do feel after doing this I am now armed with enough information to start my little book.

It may just be another chronicle of a young girl growing up in the swinging 60's, not quite on Carnaby Street or even noticing the changing times around her but managing to keep her wits together and survive through all the strange but often wonderful times being a child of the sixties provided. Aided by just a little protection from God and providence and a quirky sense of humour she managed to make it to where she is today. And where might that be you may ask? Well, all the way up the road to the Boro of course!

Chapter one

The Crow/ Cresswell road.

How the beginnings of being me all started.
I know I have a bit of a pants memory and am praying on
my hands and knees to God that this isn't the beinning of
the decline of my mental faculties, but to be fair on my
poor brain, I really don't actually remember our mam ever
telling me a great deal about how she met our dad. All I
know about the beginnings of me are that when my parents
started up together my dad had just left the Royal marines,
where he had been serving queen and country for the last
couple of years, and that he was a great catch due to him
being extremely handsome (He was, after all, one of the
three McManus brothers from Grangetown) Apart from
these snippets of information and the fact she was just 19
and he just 25 when they married, I don't really know a
great deal more about their early life together. Mind you I
have to say, there was a story about my mam's mam's
(nana Gunn) false teeth getting mixed up with my dad's
dad's (granddad McManus) false teeth on their boozed up
wedding night that was dead funny but I feel it is slightly
inappropriate to recant, due to it being quite a bit before
my time and also down to the fact it might have been made
up by our mam just for the craic.

I do believe my earliest memories to be implants, you
know the ones I mean, tales that are told to you so many
times that after a while you truly believe them to be real
memories. They are a bit like photos taken of yourself
when you were very little, photos that you have looked at

so many times you honestly, hand on heart believe you remember them being taken, even the ones of you before you got any teeth in your head or could crawl around on all fours. I know I have to be careful on this front because most of my earliest memories were given to me by my mam and remembering the entertaining person that she was, it is only fair to explain the fact that she never let the truth get in the way of a funny story. And I must admit I have a bit of a tendency to exaggerate a point to give it a more entertaining and jocular feel. So with all that in mind, I'll tell this tale to you as if it was yesterday and I remember every inch of being there.

I wasn't much more than a babe in arms when it, as in my first memory happened The whole event taking place in our small but cosy front room, where we lived at the time. The house belonged to my nana, well it was actually owned by the council but my nanas name was on the rent book, you know what I mean. The house itself was a modest mid terrace, pebble dash fronted, two up two down on the Cresswell Road in Grangetown, a small township situated close to Teesport and the iron works of Dorman Long, located really handy for the workers to get easily to and from the local industry.

It was the house I was born in and lived there with my extended family which included my older sister Karen, (who was 18 months my senior) my mam and dad, nana and grandad and uncle Bill. I lived there for about the first six months of my baby life.

Now our mam said I was only weeks old when the incident happened but I'm pretty sure I remember being reined into my big new Silvercross pram and propped up watching Bill and Ben the flowerpot men on the tiny black and white telly that was perched in the corner of the room, so I'm reckoning on being a fair bit older than that, maybe as much as four or five months old. Not that I'm going to argue with our mam's account, she has her version and I have mine and that debate is best saved for another time.

By all reckonings it was a lovely sunny day, which turned out to be a good job for all involved really as will soon become clear.

The whole event started with what can only be called a bit of a commotion on the slate roof top above the house. We could hear a whole lot of squawking, and then some shrieking, rather a bit of a racket even for this early in the afternoon. It was almost as if the big crows up there were having an almighty fight, if not a fight then they were enjoying one hell of a knees-up. One of them must have either smacked another one in the chops, or told a cracking joke that was so funny it made his pal laugh that much so as to make him lose his footing because, blimey, the next thing you know, one of them big old fellas went and fell right on down the front room chimney, (we didn't have any central heating in those days, so you can see why it was a good job it was a sunny day, this story would have had a whole different ending if the fire had been burning in the grate.)

Well, that crow came flapping down that chimney in the biggest cloud of soot you ever laid your sweet little eyes on, (we weren't the type to have a chimney sweep come in and give it a clean, a handful of salt chucked up it was as close as that chimney ever came to a service), and me, being parked smack bang in the middle of the room in my swanky new Silvercross pram got the best eyes view ever. Boy was that a blooming big crow, as least as big as me, hell, it was as big as our Kaz. Mind you being the little minx I was, I wasn't even a bit frightened just slightly perplexed and interested to watch what would unfold, I still wasn't scared when it shook its feathers, regained it's composure, and decided the best way out wasn't back up the chimney and began flapping frantically round the room trying to find an exit.

In the midst of all this hullabaloo, our mam, being of the self preservation mind set, 'it's all about me,' being the lifetime motto she lived by and passed on to me. (Being the good daughter that I am I have taken it to heart and also stand by her precious motto.) She grabbed my big sister and bolted at lightning speed for the door, cleared the hall in record time arriving in the safety of the open air in a time Peter Radford, bronze medal winner of the 1960's Olympics would have eaten his own ear to match.

Without a thought for anyone but herself she escaped (okay, she did have the presence of mind to snatch up our Karen) but she just abandoned poor little old me to fend off the maniac crow single handed. And that crow by now had a bit of a concussion after bashing it's stupid head against the front room window in an effort to escape. I could see the panic in it's beady little eyes as it tried to register why it couldn't get through the glass. A trickle of blood was now starting to dribble down its shiny black beak and spattered the room when it whirled around to find another exit.

I don't quite know who saved my sorry little botty, but I'm pretty sure it wasn't our mam because my clear true memory of the day was of her, standing in the front garden of the house, hands flat on the window and face pressed up against the glass, eyes wild, mouth wide open and screaming at me not to panic, everything was going to be fine, all of this whilst our Kaz whaled like a walrus tucked under mams shaky arm. Give mam her dues, she did look - totally frazzled, and more than slightly worried for my life, but not enough to put her own in danger by rescuing me. Well, it all turned out to be alright in the end, the crow was set free, mam came in, it took her the rest of the afternoon to clean up all the sooty mess in nana's front room. I had managed to be modestly entertained by the crows adventure in front-room-land which was only fair as I had, after all, missed Bill and Ben the flower pot men and didn't even get a glimpse of my favourite character, Little Weed!

Okay, I admit, I might not remember it all that clearly, but our mam's face at the window bit is all true! And I know this for sure because I have no photos of this event to prompt a memory and our mam would never in a million years admit that she had abandoned me to the clutches of that big old crow and do the twenty yard dash in half a second flat in favour of the safety of the front garden.

My next earliest memory (this may also be one of those dodgy implants) moves on a bit in time to around about the March of '63. I was as per usual in my baby life, strapped in my reins in my prison that disguised itself and a swanky pram again. I don't think I was set free from those reins until our Gary came along to take centre stage in them. I am, at this place in time about 6 months old and the country has just experienced the Big Freeze of 1963, when record snowfall and plunging temperatures brought the country to a halt.

The Cresswell Road wasn't exactly on a par with the leafy suburbs and Grangetown was not what you would exactly call idyllic middle England (I think it's twinned with Beirut, seriously) but, this was where we lived and it was proper council house living in all it's wonderful glory. Bearing this in mind I can tell you it wasn't an unusual occurrence for mam to push me out in the pram whatever the weather. This being due to the fact we couldn't afford a car and if you needed something getting from the shops it was on your feet or the bus and my swanky Silver cross pram was too big to get up the step on to the bus, so pushing me it usually was. In our dads defence not that many folks could afford to buy a car in the 60's and there were much more important priorities, i.e. booze, fags and bingo.

Fortuitously that day, the sun had decided to come out and it seemed a nice enough day for mam to pop to the post office and get nana's pension and a few bits and bobs from the shop. I can see you're wondering where I'm going with this one, but bare with me just for a little bit and it will all start to make sense.

Now back in the 60's times were a bit different than they are today and folks were not quite as paranoid about their babies being pinched out of their prams, so it was a common enough sight to see the odd one parked outside the shops, or the post office or the bingo, or wherever it was your mam was visiting, and if she was a bit of a gob-a-lot like mine was then chances are you could be parked there for quite some time, especially if she bumped into a neighbour/friend/ someone she barely knew who she felt needed to know her life story.

I spent a lot of time parked outside shops, but our mam always propped me up so I could see what was occurring around me to keep me entertained. I was a bit of a nosey parker when I was a baby, and if she didn't prop me up, I would scream like a banshee and spoil her gossiping.

Did I mention that it had been the worse winter on record with record snowfall and freezing temperatures? I must admit this didn't bother me much, because trying to wriggle out of that straightjacket known as the reins I spent so much of my baby life in, warmed you up rather nicely. In fact it got pretty hot under that glaring sun that had decided to pop its head out.

As it turns out rising temperatures and bright sunshine are a lethal combination for shifting large packs of compressed snow from post office roofs and down onto unsuspecting young victims.

I wish I could have seen our mam's face when she eventually emerged from the post office after what must have been some ear ache she gave the poor clerk, her tired jaw must have dropped hard enough to crack when she found her precious Silvercross pram under a small mountain of the white not so fluffy stuff, which by all accounts took quite some time to dig through. Alas, all I can remember is the cosy white igloo the hood of my pram and the snow forged lovingly all around me. Those Silvercross prams, by heck, they were built for business!

Chapter two

The Big Move

The big move story is a bit of a family legend, we all have them in our histories, the stories that get bigger every time you tell them, you know the ones, like how big the stickle back fish was that you caught in Stewart Park lake using just a worm, some grubby old string and a couple of hours careful patience. You reluctantly had to chuck it back in the water because you thought you might be asked by the conductor to pay full fare for it on the 63 bus you would be catching on the way back home, this being due to the fact it looked like it might take up a whole seat to itself. Well that stickleback started off quite big but by the time you told the story about it to your fifth friend, it had grown to 27 foot long, with sparkling white teeth and could sing like Elvis. That sort of thing, it's the Chinese whispers effect. Well, family legends are kind of like in that same vein. And with all this in mind, taking in to account this story has been told to us by our mam more times than I care to remember I will begin the McManus family legend which is the Big Move story.

So, you already know by now that I was born in my nanas council house in Grangetown and that literally was where I was born, in my mam and dads double bed in the back bedroom of Cresswell Road, not Parkside maternity home where most babies made their first appearance if you lived on Teesside. Even in the sixties this was a bit odd as most folks managed to get to the hospital in time for the arrival, but it turns out I was in a bit of a rush to get into the world (I'm still quite impatient, okay, for those of you that know me who are reading this, actually very impatient) and I ended up being delivered by my dad's Aunty Chris who had had loads of kids herself and would have even more in the future, and one of nanas neighbours who knew the ropes because she'd delivered a couple of puppies to a stray dog that had wandered into her back garden shed just a few weeks earlier.

Uncle Billy was one of the first to grace the scene, and popped his handsome thickly covered mop of a head in the room to get a good look at his lovely new niece. To this days he still describes me as looking like a little baby monkey, all of this, according to uncle Bill, being due to the fact my hair started growing a millimetre above my eyebrows and was thick and as black as his own. I think uncle Bill, like myself, had a bit of a tendency to exaggerate no one's hair starts growing there! If you ask me? And going by the photos, I was cute as!

Uncle Billy is my dad's younger brother, who still lived at home with his mam and dad, the more I think of it, the more that little council house is starting to fill up big style and I'm trying to work out where abouts we all slept. Anyways, Uncle Billy runs all the way down to the social club at the end of town near the steel works and gets my dad, who in turn runs all the way back to the house to see his second born daughter.

"My God! Look at all that lovely black hair! She's a proper McManus she is" Our dad was dead proud and puffed his chest out like a peacock.

Now in Grangetown, in 1962, no one owned such a thing as a telephone, and even if they did my dad was a proud man and would never have put upon his neighbours to have a borrow of it, but he wanted to tell his older brother Don about the gorgeous little girl his Maureen had just given birth to, so he decided to run all the way to South Bank and tell Uncle Don in person. (about 5 miles in all). I need to stop the story here and give you a bit of background information on Uncle Don so you can get the gist of the 'Big move story'.

Uncle Don was dads older brother by 5 years, I always thought he was okay, in fact I always thought he was really nice. He moved to Oz when I was a little kid so I can't say I knew him all that well, but from stories told to me as I was growing up, I got the impression he was a bit of a snob, but in a nice way. Uncle Billy told me he used to lock him and our dad in the little back bedroom and subject them to hours of classical music played at full volume to drill some sophistication into them. He would also make them read the classics instead of comics, teach them to speak properly instead of with a Middlesbrough twang in the hope that they would, like him become more cultured and refined, that sort of thing.

Anyways, he met a lovely German girl, Renate*, courted her for a short while then married her and moved over to South Bank, the next town down from ours. Blooming good job too if you ask me, or we'd have all been in bunk beds, top and tail and eating our dinner in sittings whilst bursting out of my nanas house!

Well, our dad overcome with pride, runs all the way over to South Bank, knocks on their door in a bit of a lather, panting and catching his breath and what do you know, Uncle Don's only gone and moved without telling anyone!! The blooming big snob!

I imagine you're thinking, 'so what, that's not such a big move, you've certainly built this story up bigger than it is, but that's not it, the Big Move Story, I haven't got there yet. I don't quite know if you can see where I'm going with this but I will persist.

By now Cresswell road is getting pretty full, what with nana, granddad, Uncle Billy, mam, dad, our Kaz and now little old me all squeezed into what basically was a two up, two down street house. (I just asked our Kaz about that and it turns out it had a teeny tiny box room too, that was where Uncle Bill slept, phew, I had visions of him in the airing cupboard there for a while.)

Well, the council in all it's great wisdom, decides to give our mam and dad their very own place, and what luck do they have? Not only is it in Redcar, dead posh compared to Grangetown, what with it being on the coast and not so close to the works, but it's a brand spanking new three bed roomed council house with a garden, the latest in aluminium window frames, fitted kitchen units (all two of them,) indoor plumbing and a concrete garden shed, and get this, no loo in the garden, and on the Lakes estate, at Redcar, even the name, The Lakes estate sounded posh. They couldn't believe their good fortune and would have loved to go round to uncle Don's to brag, but as I said earlier, he'd moved.

Now I did say this was a family legend but I forgot to mention that it came from my mam, as entertaining a story teller you could ever meet, so again I have to add that there may be absolutely no truth in it what so ever. I'm pretty sure quite a few of her yarns were fictional, but never mind that, it's still a craicing story.

Our mam was never a fan of Uncle Don and Aunty Renate's. She liked to call them 'those snobby relatives,' who thought they were better than the rest of us and liked to look down their noses at us scruffy lot. Every family has some by all accounts. You know the ones. They want to do better for themselves, aspire to be someone, improve themselves, they like the sophisticated finer things in life, that sort of thing. So the vane this story was told to me, coming from our mam, might have just a slightly bias slant against the pair of them.

Well, the big day comes. Our little family gets the keys to our new home, waves tara to nana, granddad, Uncle Billy and all the old neighbours, and moves what meagre belongings we own to 32 Rutland Close, our dream home, in posh Redcar, on the coast, with a garden and new posher neighbours, the Simmons, who, by the way, moved into their house a couple of weeks after us on a horse and cart, Classy!

We say 'Bon voyage' to our previous life in Grangetown because moving to Redcar means we're on the up.

Weeks go by, and we're all starting to settle in nicely, mam's finding her feet, getting to know where the shops are, where the schools are, more importantly where the nearest bingo is.

Dad's already a member of the local social club, The Lakes, he's on the billiards team and even managed to have a tab started.

When what do you know? Who does our mam only go and bump into on the Mersey road, not two minutes from where we now live, like an amazing bolt out of the blue? She only goes and bumps into aunty Renate at the bus stop waiting to catch the 263 into town.

"Oh, My giddy aunt! Do my eyes deceive me? Is that you Renate?" our mam asks as she pushed me along strapped once again into my silver cross pram, which is looking not so swanky and a bit worse for wear after the igloo incident. She hardly came up for air, "fancy bumping into you here on the Mersey road in Redcar of all places, how bizarre is that, you'll never guess in a month of Sundays Renate, but we only went and got a brand new fabulous council house on the Lakes estate after I had our Susan here." She takes a break to catch her breath and point me out to Renate, who in turn, took a quick glance in the pram and was impressed with how gorgeous I was with all my lovely black hair which didn't grow from just above my eyebrows, thank you very much Uncle Billy!!!

"Mac ran all the way to South Bank, non stop, to tell you both about her being born, but when he got there, you'd only gone and up sticks and moved."

Now this is the bit I missed because I'd almost wriggled one of my arms out of the strap of my straight jacket and could almost sniff freedom, so I can't say I was paying full attention, but that didn't matter much, because our mam told this story to us a hundred times or more, in what I can only call a really bad attempt at imitating a German with a hint of Gestapo accent (family legend remember.)

According to the great impersonator Maureen aka our mam, Aunty Renate replied in her 'most snobbiest oh la la' of voices "Yes, ve moved here to get avay from you blooming scruffy lot!"

Fair to say the next move they made was to make sure we never followed and took them all the way around the other side of the world to Oz!

* Aunty Renate, was Uncle Dons wife and I have to tell you this about her because it always makes me giggle. Bless his little cotton socks, but our Gary always got her

name mixed up with Nancy Sinatra's, (how way, say them both out loud to yourself and it's easy to see why! And in his defence he was only dead little at the time) whenever Frank's famous singing daughter made an appearance on the telly singing about them boots that were made for walking, the ones that were going to walk all over you, well, his little face would light up he would become all animated and shout her name…Aunty Renate, Aunty Renate. God love him.

Chapter three

The Lakes Estate (AKA The Closes)

Now in 1965, 20 years after World War two and Britain had regained it's footing and was on the up, the new garden cities were emerging all over the country and none so better than the Closes, so called because all the houses were built to enclose a large forecourt style space, or maybes because they were all closes. I. e. Rutland Close, Kent Close, Essex Close, yes, you get the picture. Anyways it turned out to be a crap design, especially for the bin men, who, by the way, were real men in those days, hauling the steel bins onto their muscular broad shoulders and running with them at break neck speed across those crappily designed forecourts. And when folks started to be able to afford to drive around in cars, the number of fights that broke out over parking spaces was unbelievable. It just goes to show, there was no forward thinking from Redcar crappy Council, who thought us council house plebs would never amount to being able to afford a car. Rant over! But, boy, oh boy, did we fit in, The McManus's. Our dad worked at the local ICI plant at The Wilton Works as a process operator, I still to this day have no clue as to what a process worker was but it brought a wage home and we always had a roof over our heads and food on the table, well almost always. When not at work, most of his spare time was spent at the Lakes social club, with either a pint or a snooker club in hand. (He told me he once got a 147*, but I'm thinking this was maybe another one of them family legends or at least when the story started it was a 47 but just got bigger with each telling).

Our mam, by now had three kids under school age, our Gary popping out in September '63, not even a year after me, this in a time when there wasn't much on the telly so other forms of entertainment produced big families. Well, she was a stay at home mam, mind you she did have the odd part time job when times were extra hard, but her main role in life whilst we were growing up was big style gossip. Nothing that went on in the Closes got past her, and she felt it was her gossipy mare duty to add a little flavour to the tittletattle, juicy it up a bit and then pass it on, getting her in to bother on more than one occasion.

Due to this amazing career of hers, most of my early years were spent round neighbours houses. Aunty Joyce, Aunty Steph, Aunty Flossy, what-do-you-know all of our mam's friends turned out to be our aunties.

And a great deal of my oldest memories centre around the back gardens of these lovely ladies, whose kids became my closest of friends. Next doors, or Aunty Joyce's, being where my bessa friend lived. Stephen Simmons**. We shared many a good laugh, sometimes a good howl and even the odd sandwich. (Usually his with me, rarely the other way round). I spent the whole of one summer trying to teach him how to knit, now that's real friendship for you.

But the McManus family almost became ostracised by the Simmons on the fateful day our Karen cut Glen's hair, Glen being Stephen's youngest brother.

Now I know what you're thinking here, all kids do that, what's the big drama? My own daughter not only cut a big chunk of her hair all the way down to the scalp, then continued to take the scissors to the unsuspecting curtains and demolished them too, after that she decided to shave her tongue with a Bic disposable razor, and couldn't speak for a week because it swelled up in her mouth so much. Kids do stuff like, because they can, just to see what will happen, and to make their mam's freak out when they see what's been done.

But you really have to get this hair cutting event into context.

The Simmons family were an average size family compared to some in the Closes, Jeffrey, the oldest, then Stephen, then Barry, after him came little Glen, and a few years later out popped baby Dawn, but the hair cutting event happened when Dawn was just a babe or she might have suffered the same ill fate. Oh yeah, and they had a dog called Tuppence, I think in total they had five dogs, one after the other, all called Tuppence. And they all used to eat the left over potato peelings instead of dog food when times were hard, I kid you not!

Now, if you asked our Karen to tell you this same story her version of it will be quite different from mine, but that possibly has to do with the fact that she paid a lot more attention to general stuff whilst growing up than I did, I tended to daydream a lot and then fill in the missing bits with a more entertaining and amusing version of events. I get that from my mam, who like I said earlier never let the truth get in the way of a good story.

It was a lovely scorcher of a day, the sun was belting down from the clear blue skies above, not a whiff of cloud for miles. Just like most of the days from my childhood. Our mam was yakking in Joyce's back kitchen and we were all at play in the Simmons's back garden. Not that it was much of a garden mind, I don't even think they had any grass, just mud, a few weeds and a concrete path which ran from the gate right the way up to the ever open back kitchen door.

I don't remember where the scissors came from, but one minute our Karen's hands were empty, the next she was Kazza Snippy Fingers with a queue of kids a mile long, all lined up, patiently waiting to get the latest hair do's. (Not me though, due to the fact I didn't want to catch the dreaded nits, so always had a very short bowl on the head style crop).

I think Stephen went first, snip, snip, snip, snip, snip, "Oh my, doesn't he look like George Harrison from the Beatles," someone was heard to say.

"Do me next!" shouted Paul Firman, from next-door-but-one, and what do you know, up popped another Beatle, Paul McCartney this time. By heck, she might only be five but god can our Kazza cut hair! Well she moved down that row of waiting customers like Vidal Sassoon on a bike, bestowing on them all the latest do's, Elvis's quiff, Cliff's fringe, mullets galore, until she got to Glen. Now here lies the crux of the story. Glen Simmons was, and we all knew it, Joyce's favourite child, her baby. He was a sweet little kid, a couple of years younger than me, but unlike me, he only had about four hairs growing from the top of his extremely hair free bonce. Now I'm pretty sure our Karen, in all her five year old wisdom, thought that if she cut them off, ten would grow in their place and by this time next year Glen would have a marvellously full mullet. So she was pretty proud of herself by the time our mam and Joyce came into the garden after a couple of hours yakking over a gallon of tea. Now this parts a bit of a blur to me, possibly caused by the 100 decibel scream that came from Joyce's wide open gob making my head go a bit bong, or the whirlwind speed she ran past me down that concrete path to save the last two hairs on Glen's poor head, or even by the gale force wind caused by the flapping of her skinny arms as she grabbed her baby out of the clutches of the demon Sweeny Todd that was our Karen.

"Don't worry Joyce" I remember our mam trying to calm her good friend and next door neighbour, as Joyce clutched to her chest her 'bereft of hair' baby and cradled his small head in her hands, "It'll grow back in a couple of weeks, honestly, you'll see", but, as you can guess by the magnitude of this story, it never did! Glen Simmons was about five years old before he had a half decent head of hair and even then it wasn't really up to very much, not like my beautiful head of glossy black hair that didn't grow from just above my eyebrows, Uncle exaggerator Bill, okay, okay I'll drop it now!

It must have cost a small fortunes in hats, keeping his little baldy head warm in the winter. And of course it was all that 'scheming little minx Karen McManus' from next-doors fault, and we all got tarred with that same shame-on-you-lots hairbrush.

Lucky for me Stephen liked his do and we managed to stay bessa friends right up until I dumped him after we moved from the Closes when I was about 9. Fickle I know, but a girl's got to move with the times.

* For those of you not in the snooker know, a 147 is when all the balls are pocketed in the highest sequence by a single person in a single turn. It is the highest score you can get at snookers, akin to 180 in darts. Do I have to explain darts, nah just leave it at that.

** Stephen Simmons was picked as my bessa friend for a number of reasons.

a) He lived next-door, easy access.

b) He was a good laugh, could spin a good yarn and had a repertoire of crappy jokes.

c) He shared, we were both second siblings and this is suppose to make you good at sharing, I seemed to have missed out on that trait.

d) And best of all, he was special, not in a way that most folks would have cared but to me it made him stand out from the rest, and what you may ask made him so special? Well he had 3 thumbs, how good was that, the thumb on his right hand had a little tiny baby thumb growing out of the side. It never ceased to amaze me and I would always ask Stephen to show me it up close and personal so I could gawp in wonder at it, that thumb would mesmerise me every glance I got right up until the operation to remove it, when I must say Stephen did lose a little bit of his sparkle.

e) Just had a word with our Gaz and he reminded me that Stephen was a mint Yodeller, he used to try and teach us all how to yodel like an knickerbocker wearing Austrian or his idol Frank Ifield, not of us were a patch on Stephen....I can't believe I forgot that.

Chapter four

Sunday Night

The Closes produced quite a few family legends, and I'll try my best to recall them all as clearly and honestly as I can, but this early time in my life was also full of rituals that were religiously repeated, these are also worthy of recording, as they help paint a picture of our family life, a life that has long since been left in the past and with a bit of luck will stay that way. One of the more notable of these rituals was Sunday night.

At the end of each week came the weekend, oh the joy! The freedom, no school, playing out with my pals until dark, walking for hours up to Gypsy woods with not much more than a Lowcocks lemonade bottle filled with lukewarm water and a squashed jam sandwich in my cardigan pocket, bliss! Endless hours of fun swinging on an old tyre someone had tied to a length of thick rope and slung over a branch of a big old Sycamore tree, it was the best tarzee for miles and afforded me many hours of unbridled pleasure as I swung across the shallow beck it hung above.

But at the end of every weekend came Sunday night, AKA bath night.

Okay, I can now see why I had to have a bath once a week, there was, after all, quite a bit of mud to be covered in when you fell from that tarzee and into that beck. But the idea of what was coming, lingered low in the back of your head taking the sparkle off the lovely time away from school whilst you enjoyed your freedom.

It was a bit like when a bluebottle landed on the rare ice cream cornet you managed to afford. It tucked into a bit of the creamy loveliness then flew off, you knew it had landed there and tried not to think about the last place it had visited beforehand, (because we all knew where their favourite place to land is, yuk!) and just enjoy your cornet anyway. But there was no escaping the thoughts about that fly as they went through your little head. Just like bath night, you tried your best to ignore it and not let it spoil the yummy delicious enjoyment.

Sunday Night/Bath Night! I hated it! Apart from anything else there was the dreaded Coal Tar soap*, the smell of which still lingered all over your skin from the previous weeks bath night. And no such thing as shampoo, not in the McManus household, again the dreaded Coal Tar soap, rock hard on your sopping wet head as your mam scrubbed the dried in dirt from your scalp and tried to bludgeon to death any nitty walkers** that had the audacity to try and inhabit your hair. If that wasn't bad enough you had to get in the tub after your mam, who, just for the craic, would announce every fart she did that bubbled up through the water just in case you didn't get a good sniff of it when you climbed in.

Then, like it couldn't even get any worse, you had to get in the water with both your sister and your brother. I must have been about ten years old before I had the pleasure of a bath on my own.

In the winter it was worse, we only ever ran the hot tap into the tub during the cold spell, and yes, it did a pretty good job of providing warm water, but the tub itself seemed to be totally oblivious to the heat, your little bum cheeks always managing to touch the cold metal as you stepped over the side and then plonked yourself down in the water. The bathroom itself was so cold, it steamed up like a sauna and you could barely see your hand in front of your face. Once in the tub you would try and tuck as much of yourself under the warm water as was humanly possible without drowning. This to try and stop the Goosebumps rising all over your skin, alas, all these antics managed to do was cause a big fight between you and your siblings who were both also trying to do the same.

When your mam deemed you to be clean enough and ponged enough of coal tar soap that you were allowed to get out, you were confronted by another commotion and dilemma.

a) Do I want to get dry on the only bath sheet we own, which our mam has just used, it maybe sopping wet with a whiff of stale farts, but at least it covered you from head to toe and stopped the water freezing on your skin or,

b) use one of the other dry towels we owned, ones that our dad had nicked from work with ICI printed all the way through the weave, they may be dry and did a better job of soaking the water off your skin but they were about as big as the average flannel and didn't even go near covering your bits and bobs and you never knew which of the neighbours kids would be waiting outside the door to get in after you.

Right, you're thinking, she's made it through the ritual that was having a bath in Rutland Close, that wasn't so bad, what is she whinging about, but worse it yet to come, the memory of which, even to this day, sends shivers up and down my spine and makes my scalp tingle.

The dreaded NITTY COMB!!!!!!!!, the worst tool of torture ever invented, sharp, cold, metal, totally inflexible and dragged sharply through your wet hair to rid you of every child of the 60's number one enemy known as the nits.

And there was no such thing as conditioner to softer your hair in those days, and smooth the passage of the comb through your locks, no such luck.

You were grabbed by your ears, clasped between your mam's meaty thighs, and yes, the farty smell still lingered there too, and then you were, what I can only describe as tortured with the little instrument of pure pain until your mam decided you were after all Nit free and released from her clutches.

Now I always had my bowl-on-the-head style hairdo because I wanted this process to be over ASAP and I wasn't a bit bothered if I looked like a little lad, but our Karen, bless her, loved her long hair and had to suffer at least an extra two minutes of torture with that comb for the privilege of having these flowing locks. She did, however, pay the price for them. On more than one occasion her flowing tresses were invaded by the little blood sucking hitchhikers and she had to endure the torture of bath night and the nitty comb, every night of the week. She also had to endure the humiliation of being sent home from school by the nitty nurse with the 'horror of horrors' that was the nitty letter! To this day she still tells me how she was mentally scarred for life after having had to do the nitty-walk-of-shame over to Norma Holmes's house, (Norma being an ace nit killer), her hair covered in stinky Dermabac shampoo and her head held low with the utter shame of it all. And of course there were the physical scars when she got a good battering from our mam with the hair brush for getting them in the first place.

So the ritual that was Sunday night/ bath night may be a bit of a stain on my memory, but I'm thinking that it is possibly a stain and a half on my sisters. Thankfully after years of being able to get a bath any night of the week the trauma has passed.

 * Coal tar soap, actually Wrights Coal tar soap was a popular brand of antiseptic soap, popular due to the fact that it was the cheapest soap available, there were loads of other varieties at the time, Lifebuoy, Shields and Fairy, but not for us, according to our mam when you smelled of Coal tar soap, you smelled clean.

** Nitty walkers are the Closes name for Head lice with legs. Head lice were a common affliction most of us Closes kids got whilst growing up, I bet quite a few of you lot reading this had them too, mind you, I never once got them as a kid and I think this demonstrates that the bowl on the head 'do' I had did the trick, I waited until I was fully grown with three kids of my own before I had the displeasure of a visit from the dreaded little lice, and it was utterly mortifying.

There are 2 types of nits that inhabit your hair, the eggs, that glue themselves to your hair, which the Nittycomb is used to dislodge and kill, and the Walkers, that wander around your head laying the eggs and sucking your blood causing your head to be really itchy, but when these

Walkers are caught and squashed between both thumb nails, they crack with the most satisfying of noises.

Chapter five

The Open Fire

Staying with the theme of rituals, one of my clear memories from growing up in the Closes isn't so much as a ritual, more of a regular occurrence, actually not so much a regular occurrence as a day to day necessity.

The Closes were newly built when we moved into our house in 1962 but you have to remember, this isn't a swanky 3 bed roomed semi, like Uncle Dons and Aunty Renate's place (or should I say Nancy Sinatra's , I'm going to give our Gary a copy of this book. Hehe) It is, after all a council house, and even though it was brand new it didn't come with all the mod cons that were constantly being introduced in the sixties. We were well impressed with being in possession of an indoor loo and hot running water which was heated by switching on the Immersion heater that was housed in the airing cupboard at the top of the stair, it was still lacking in what most houses of the times lacked, and we would feel aggrieved without today, good old central heating (don't you just love it!). Most of the neighbours were the same, all relying on the coal fire. There was, of course, the odd one of means who could afford the luxury that was a two bar electric fire, but not us.

So the only method of heating the house in the cold weather was by firing up the coal fire in the front room, and to be fair that fire tried its best and did manage to make the front room lovely and toasty, but as soon as you stepped outside of that room, well it was like a trip to the Artic, and up the stairs in the winter was blooming Baltic, our Kaz used to wear her vest, knickers, nighty, dressing gown, hat, socks and a cardy to bed to try and keep warm, and when she got up in the morning she managed to get changed into her school uniform whilst still under the heavy blankets, it was a bit like watching the telly when Harry Houdini was trying to escape from a straight-jacket. In the winter the fire was constantly kept lit but left to dull down over night with just a couple of cones of sea-coal thrown on it, to try and stop it from going out.

Now to get that fire up and roaring the next morning, is by all accounts a precise and exacting art form, according to our Gary, who was an absolute champion at it from about the tender age of about five. After a while our mam started to hide the matches out of sight from him, chuntering something under her breath about him being a bit of a pyromaniac who didn't contain his fire starting talents to the grate, I had no idea what that meant at the time and thought she was just showing off that she knew a fancy new word.

But boy, could he get those flames to lick up that chimney. He said the trick was to cause a vacuum by balancing the small wooden handled coal shovel between the lower grate of the fire and the top edge of the fireplace. This would then anchor in place a page from the daily newspaper that was spread right across the whole of the front of the fire. Then you had to watch carefully as the fire took hold, the paper would begin to be sucked in very slightly as the air was drawn up through the bars in the grate below, the whole process was mesmerising to watch as small dark brown circles would appear on the newspaper, these circles would start to grow bigger and bigger and the centre of them would get darker and darker, until they would suddenly burst into flames and were sucked up the chimney causing tiny flutters of glowing burning paper to scatter and be blown around the front room. Then you had to make sure that none of these floaters had landed on the furniture or got caught in the rug in front of the fire or the whole place would go up in flames. Some stamping out was sometimes required but we never had a full on 'the rugs on fire' moment, but it did look pretty scruffy with all the black burn marks.

If there wasn't enough suction to get the vacuum to form and pull the newspaper in, this often being due to too much ash blocking the in 'need of a clean' grate, Our Gary would then have to hunker down on all fours with his lips puckered up near the grate and blow with all his little five year old might, and if this also wasn't enough to get that fire roaring then he would sometimes have to resort to nipping in the kitchen for a handful of sugar to sprinkle on the hot coals, to really fire it up. He somehow always manage to get us warmed up in the morning and on the evening he would go to great lengths to keep the fire built up, then after all his hard work he would spend hours just staring into the flames, sometimes we'd get the forks from the cutlery drawer and hang a piece of bread on them to toast in the flames often burning our hands, but it was worth it, the smokey flavour of that toast done on the open fire just couldn't be beaten, delicious.

Do you know I've just had a thought, numerous small fires were set all over the estate, in gardens and sheds when we lived there, nobody was hurt but quite a few pounds worth of damage was done, and the culprit never did get caught. Nah, it couldn't have been? No way, he was only five!

Chapter six

Die, Sparrow, Die

Nobody ever had a sister as caring as our Karen was, she always looked out for me throughout my childhood and received as many a good hidings as I did simply because she couldn't hide the disgust on her face at our mam when I was getting one. My good hidings were almost always well earned, I was a bit of a swine most of the time. But not our Karen, she tried really hard to be a good girl and succeeded most of the time.

Any wounded animal, any stray, any tramp with a shaggy dog story and she'd bring them home. Her heart was as big as the moon. But she never learned the hardest of lessons. You had to be pretty fortuitous to make it out of our house alive or at least in one piece. The McManus family should have come with a tagline, not good with pets. Not that we ever deliberately hurt any of them, we all liked them, it just seemed that as soon as they were carried over the door step of our humble abode that they were doomed. Take for instant the very first pet/victim that I recall being brought home to our house. It was a baby sparrow, only a couple of weeks old, it barely had any feathers on it's scrawny little body and had obviously fell out of its nest, unluckily for the poor thing, straight into the path of Saint Karen. We were on our way home from school at the time, St Albans Roman Catholic Infant School just off the Low Farm drive. Not a bad school really, but quite a walk home when you're only five and your big six year old sister insists on stopping for every Tom, Dick or Sparrow. And if I remember rightly, I was absolutely starving, well to be honest I was always absolutely starving on the way home from school after spending the whole day trying to be good, which is really hard work when you're only five and being good isn't your forte, it uses up lots of calories and wares a girl out. So I was best not pleased with the delay my sister was making with the whole 'save a sparrow' routine. Not only did we have to stop and pick the squawking little thing up, but we also spent ten minutes trying to find some tissue to wrap it up in to make sure it was warm and snug for the journey home. I think she even tried a bit of birdie CPR on its little chest whilst blowing in its little yellow beak. Okay, I might have made that bit up for dramatic effect, but I wouldn't have put it past her she was so dedicated. Now my sister is all grown up, guess what she is? A Nurse, well, what a surprise!

After carefully placing it in her pocket, wrapped is someone's discarded newspaper that had been reused for wrapping someone else's chips in, with congealed chip fat all over it, we walked home at a snail's pace so as to make the journey as stress free as possible for the poor little thing, which was now all covered in chip fat, and safely ensconced in her coat pocket. And to make the journey even slower she insisted on stopping every five minutes just to check on it.

"Aw come on Kaz, hurry up! I'm starving here!" I wasn't at all a bit self-centred as a kid, me like. And I didn't mind letting everyone know how I was feeling. Our Kaz just tutted at me and gently waved her finger in my face to shut me up, all my whinging was disturbing the little patient in her pocket.

Well it was a blooming long journey home but, lordy lord, what do you know, I can hardly believe my eyes? Our mam's in! That makes a refreshing change from having to knock on all the aunties doors after school, and find which

one of them she was having a bit of a chin wag and a brew
with. And, hang fire, is that the smell of tea being cooked
coming from the back kitchen? Blimey, is it my birthday
or something?

"What time do you call this? You should have been home
ages ago you little beggers, get in here quick your tea is
getting cold!" Quick as a flash, with no need to be told
twice, I'm at the table woofing mine down.

"What's that you've got in your pocket there?" I remember
our mam asking as our Karen removed the little sparrow
all wrapped in greasy newspaper from her coat pocket. It
had livened up a bit and was actually looking rather perky.
When our mam saw it, she rolled her eyes in her head, then
smiled, no one could have failed not to have thought that
little bird looked really cute, with its ruffles feathers and
dazed look on its face.

"Aw give it here while you get your tea girl" she said.
Our Karen handed it over to be looked after by our mam.
We watched her, as we scoffed our tea down, gently place
the little baby bird in some tinfoil.

"It's freezing cold, poor little thing" she said it with such
care, "I'm just going to pop it in the bottom of the grill it
will still be a bit warm in there after your tea, that should
get the little thing feeling better."

Well, what can I say, we were dead impressed, our mam,
the birdie nurse, seems to know what she's doing, getting
it warmed up, we'll just enjoy our fish fingers and let her
take charge. (I don't think they were Bird's eye fish fingers
but they were blooming delicious with the big plate of
bread and butter, well, actually bread and Stork margarine,
we had with them.)

And in no time at all we had finished and made our way
into the kitchen to check up on the patient.

It really doesn't take a rocket scientist to see how this sorry little tale ends, as it turned out our dosey mam had only gone and forgot to switch the grill off. The temperature in there was well above a nice warming up, and what with the little darling being covered in chip fat it didn't stand a cat-in-hells chance, it came out done to a T, with smoke coming from underneath the foil, or maybes it was steam, the kitchen filling with a aroma of cooked bird (smelled a bit like Sunday dinner when we had chicken) and I even think mam burned her fingers in her hurry to unwrapping the foil from around the done to a crisp remains of the McManus family first victim.

Chapter seven

Learn To Swim Young Girl, Learn To Swim.

All the McManus family members dating back to Shamus the fish in 1055bc, have been amazing swimmers and none of them better than our dad. I don't know how much of a regular swimmer he was when we were little kids, but I do remember how he used to go to Redcar swimming baths every single day after he retired. It was quiet the joke in the family because he was as tight as the proverbial ducks posterior and never once paid to get in.

At Redcar baths the attendants on the door only took a quick look at your ticket, which was purchased at the bowling alley on the other side of the road, but never actually collected them in.

After folks had finished their swim it was quite common to see them exit the building and then discard their ticket either in the bin provided or just on the road outside. Our dad, always on the look-out for an opportunity to save himself a penny or two, would pick up one of these discarded tickets, sometimes having to resort to rummaging through the bins, and offer it up as his own, never once did he have to pay to get in, the crafty old sod he was.

He may have not been the best husband in the world, according to our mam anyways, but we thought he was the best dad ever, and still do. He was always looking out to make sure we were happy and safe growing up, and one of the things he thought was of immense importance was to make sure all of his offspring could swim, he took this very seriously and undertook to make sure we were all au fait in the water.

Our Karen and Gary are both super swimmers, but me, I'm crap, absolutely rubbish, and I owe every inch of my crappyness to the way I learned to swim.

I'm pretty sure our dad had all the best intentions in the world when he took me for my first lessons, but his natural tendencies to be a tightwad took over and to this day has had a detrimental effect on my ability, or lack of it, to swim.

Redcar baths had been built in the 1930's so had been well used by the time I frequented it in the 1960's. It was a strange old affair of a building and had originally been built with outdoor swimming too, but the wind from the seafront was known to blow the sand into the outdoor pool so that didn't last too long. The very first time I laid my eyes on it I was left with a lasting impression, for more than just its architecture.

The building sat squarely between the Majuba Road fairground and car park, the sand dunes of the beach that had a habit of letting itself be blown in your face as you approached the front doors, and the scruffy boating lake, which I fell in, (okay was pushed), once when playing 'tell your mam I saved your life.'*

The inside was proper old fashioned, but then again it was at least 30 years old, when it had been built it the 30's it had been rather swanky, but it was well and truly showing signs of wear and tear and had that shabby, in need of some TLC feeling about the place by now.

The ladies and children's changing rooms, which were always absolutely blooming freezing, even in the summer, ran the length of the right hand side of what seemed like an

Olympic sized pool, and the men's changing rooms ran all the way down the opposite side, with a viewing gallery above both areas. When you went into the changing area, the attendant handed you a huge strange metal contraption shaped like a torso with a hook at the top to hang it in storage after you had put your clothes in. Once filled, you would take it back to the attendant and exchange it for a wrist band. It weighed a tonne and being only a little dot of a five year old it was heavy going heaving it up on to the counter and handed it to the attendant to be swapped for that wristband.

But, do you know what, I didn't care one single iota, I got my clothes off, and into my hand-me-down-from-our-Karen cossy as quick as a flash, I handed that contraption over with a light heart and a head full of anticipation.

My dad was going to teach me to swim, I couldn't wait, and better still he had promised me a new rubber ring, yes a brand new rubber ring, not just armbands mind you, but a brand, spanking new rubber ring too!

I wasn't even bothered that I had just dropped my knickers in a puddle of water, and knew I was going to have a cold wet bum on the long walk all the way home. Who cares, my dad had got me a new rubber ring as well as some armbands. Get in there!

My little head was filled with images of this fabulous new rubber ring and I couldn't wait to climb in it.

Would it have little ducks all over it? What colour would it be? I hope it isn't girly pink. Will the arm bands match and not just be those bright orange glow-in-the-dark ones that everyone has?

All these thoughts were running through my head as I skipped through the disinfectant water between the changing room exit and the pool area, which was there to kill the germs and smells on folk's pongy sweaty feet. I could feel the smell of the chloride as it entered my nose making it sting and gave it a bit of a wiggle as I peered around the vast swimming area in front of me as I looked for my dad.

I could see him, exiting on the other side of the pool, his curly black hair all wet from the shower, his broad shoulders held high, the lovely smile showing his perfect white teeth, spreading across his face as he spotted me. But, hang on a minute, where was my shiny new rubber ring? And dare I even ask what was in that plastic carrier bag he was bringing with him? I felt my heart sink, it didn't bode well for me.

"Where's my new rubber ring dad?" I knew my voice sounded full of disappointment when I asked, but my anticipation slowly started to change to dread as we both stood face to face on the rough tiles at the shallow end of the pool. A sense of the inevitable, falling over me like sea fret.

"Well Susan (Aw man, please don't use my Sunday name), I was going to buy you one, but then I had a much better idea and decided my Suziwong deserves a superior swimming aid than those common old garden rubber rings from Woollies. (Woolworths for all of you born after 2000, and for all of you born after 2010, well just forget it). So I decided to make you one myself instead."

"Oh no!" my whole body sank, I can't blooming believe it "old tightwad strikes again!"

Well, he removed his homemade rubber ring from the plastic bag he'd forced it into and you could have coloured me mortified, even though I didn't know what mortified meant at four years old, I could have drawn you a Turner prize winning picture of it as I stood there on those cold wet tiles!

In my young life I'd never seen anything like it. He'd attached half a dozen polystyrene blocks around a black belt, which had a huge plastic clip fastener at the front. With lightening speed, before I could put up even the tiniest bit of a fight, he had strapped it around my little protruding belly. It was like the whole place fell into total silence, no more echoing laughter as folks jumped in the water, no splashing or shirking, I felt every set of prying eyes in the place turn and land all over me. I could feel the weight of their horror and amazement bare down on me, and the will to live was sucked straight out of my soul. The unbelievable disappointed with my not so fabulous new rubber ring and my tightwad of a dad was so immense that I decided to be done with it, those hundreds of pairs of eye on me more than I could stand, I flung myself head first into the cold chloride tasting water to end my misery and disappointment right there and then. But, what do you know, to my utter despair and amazement that ugly homemade polystyrene covered, (probably nicked from ICI) belt did a fantastic job and in an instance popped me straight back up to the surface of the water.

"That's the McManus family spirit Suziwong, what an absolutely wonderful dive that was that you just did into the water, keep flapping your little legs and arms around and you'll be a great swimmer in no time at all. In fact, I bet by the end of this first hour you'll be good enough for me to take one of the polystyrene blocks off".

"AAAAHHHGGG" Just leave me to drown!

*Tell your mam I saved your life is a game we played as kids, you'd push a pal so they thought they were going to fall into or off something they were stood near, I.e. a pool, the side of a cliff, the fire, but just before they were doomed to death or serious injury, you would pull them back thus saving their life. Quite typical of the games of the times, it sometimes went offside, I imagine quite a few kids were injured playing this game or like me ended up the victim of the person you were going to push suddenly deciding they didn't find the joke very funny. Luckily for me though this incident at Redcar boating lake happened after I had learned to swim.

Chapter eight

Eston Hills With Old Tightwad!

I'm pretty sure that when I was growing up the summer weather was much better than the summer weather that we get today. There was no better feeling than waking up in the 6 weeks holidays, being off school, and seeing the glorious day unfold through your bedroom window, watching the bright red sun come up through a cloud free sky. These skies were bluer, the clouds, when there were any, were wispier and the light summer breeze, that only sometimes blew, was just a tad warmer. There was nothing more perfect than looking forward to a summer's day with the knowledge that your dad was off work and was going to take you on a ramble all the way up Eston Hills. Especially as our dad wasn't really one for taking any time off work, (he once fell off his bike on his journey into ICI and broke his foot but still struggled on to get there. He didn't even go to the doctors until it started to turn a strange shade of black and our mam made him promise to). But when he did take his holidays he always make sure they coincided with the school holidays so that he could go rambling with his three cherished little darling kids, all the way up Eston Hills.

I don't ever remember our mam coming with us, not even once, I think she made excuses not to, so she could have some free time from us three little ankle biters and go to the bingo, maybe just sit and enjoy the peace. She really didn't know what a grand time she was missing out on.

Our dad would stride full of enthusiasm for the coming day into the bedroom, proper early and wake us all up. The breakfast would be waiting downstairs on the table for the three of us to eat after we had dressed and got down the stair. It was usually chucky eggs and soldiers which only our dad knew how to make perfectly, he always managed to keep the yolk runny and the whites nice and cooked without there being any snotty bits, the soldiers were always cut just wide enough to poke in the top of your egg without touching the shell. He would announce in a booming voice that we had to eat it all up because you needed a good feed to get you nicely ready for the long day ahead, even though it was great fun, going up Eston Hills was hard work and blooming tiring.

He'd have already packed up a bit of a picnic, usually just some Jacob's crackers, a bit of cheese and a bottle of water, or if he was feeling a bit flush, some Lowcock's lemonade, no cups, we all would take turns swigging it out of the bottle.

We'd be out of the house, quietly mind, so as not to wake out mam, on our way, and the clock hadn't even struck eight.

It was a good 3 miles hike from where we lived before you even got to the foot of Eston Hills, but the banter on the way was part of the enjoyment of the day as our dad would swing us, one at a time, on to his broad shoulders and sing little ditties to us.

"Kazza Mac is pop's lovely daughter" to our Karen.

"Suzywong is pop's lovely daughter" to me.

Our Gary didn't have a song for him so me and our Karen just assumed it was because he wasn't as lovely as us!

We'd cut through Wilton village and start our lovely day with our dad by doing a bit of 'Bird nesting.'

Now, 'bird nesting' was something we did regularly on our jolly jaunts up the hills, but now-a-days it's frowned upon.

In fact, I think it's actually illegal now to take eggs out of nests, but not when we were kids. We'd scamper round the bushes and the trees in and about the little copses around the village until we found one that we could see had a birds nest in it. Once found, we'd all holler for our dad to come over and we would watch as he reached or climbed up. Depending on how high up the nest was and if he could get to it, he would remove some of the eggs, not all of them though, our dad said it would be mean to let the mammy bird come back to an empty nest, he had a good heart like that did our dad.

He always knew which kind of bird it was too, and he would quiz us to see if we could tell by the size and colour of the egg what type of bird that had laid it. Mostly they were sparrows and starlings.

By now the sun would have really started to warm up and you could begin to feel the intense heat from it as it shone on your unprotected face and bare arms. Towards the end of the day you could clearly start to see the line where your t-shirt protected you from the sun and where your skin coloured up as it touched you. Our mam called the line around our neck that it had made the tide mark and gave it a good scrubbing with coal tar soap every Sunday to try and remove it, never with any success.

We would plod on with our journey of discovery, listening to our dad identify all the flora and fauna we passed on our way, slowly making passage up the hills until we got to the Nab. This being the very top where we always stopped to eat our picnic, and enjoy the amazing view of our town and the works that was laid bare before us. You could see the River Tees as it meandered it's way through Middlesbrough and the low lying areas, all the works were laid out in front of you, ICI, or the 'cloud making factory' as our dad liked to call it. British Steal, the red dust machine and all the estates right over to the coast at Saltburn.

By now the sun would be burning, and all three of us would try and sit on the shady side of the monument built to replace the beacon that had originally stood on the Nab, but our dad, who loved a bit of a tan, would get out a little bottle of olive oil and rub it all over his bare torso and arms to help soak up a few rays.

One of my vivid memories of him whilst growing up was the smell of his sunbathing. He would climb up on the flat shed roof in the back garden of our house in Windermere Avenue, we moved there when I was nine or ten, (because this was a good vantage spot for getting a deep tan) and would rub into his skin a concoction of olive oil, vinegar and if we had some in the house, just a smidge of lemon juice.

Whenever I treat myself to a fish supper from the local chippy and sprinkle the vinegar on my hot chips, the whiff I get up my nose as the vinegar heats up and turns to vapour takes me right back and a vision of our dad sunbathing on the roof always pops in my head. I get a warm cosy feeling that reminds me of when he would cuddle me in his big bear-hug arms in the summer.

After we'd washed our crackers and cheese down with a generous swig of pop, this done with the obligatory big burp of approval, and our dad had soaked up as much sun as his skin could stand, we would head back down the hills, usually taking a different route than the one up, to see if we could come across any new and unusual creatures or plants to identify.

I remember all these lovely long summer journeys up the hills on our days out with our sun-worshipping dad fondly, except for one.

The one where 'old tightwad dad' struck again!!

All three of us siblings adored our dad without reserve, he never failed to make us feel loved and cared for, but the one and only thing that we all found unbelievably annoying about him, was his ability to be an out and out miser. He could be generous to a fault, we were the first to have a colour telly in our street, the first to have a telephone and as soon as our mam left, the first thing he did was get central heating fitting, (he hated being cold). But on a day-to-day basis, he was tight as! Every pound was a prisoner and every penny it's guard!

It had been a warmer than average day for July when the mortifying tightwad attack happened, and we'd all enjoyed a full and fruitful day on the hills, we'd found quite a few eggs, enjoyed a picnic and scampered around the nab longer than we normally did with it being so hot and what with our dad wanting to top up his tan, so by the time we started off for home we were all feeling rather tired. In fact, by the time we got to the bottom of the hills the three of us were falling off our little feet, even our fit as a fiddle dad, who's favourite saying was 'don't worry your little head about me, I'll outlive the lot of you' had to give in and admit he was tired.

"Can we get the bus the rest of the way please dad?" We all pleaded. We knew it was a bit of a long shot, but pulled faces expressing our tiredness to emphasis our plight. It was, after all, instilled in all three of us that feet were made for travelling on and the bus was a big old luxury. But to our amazement his answer was yes, all we could think was that his sunburn must have been pretty bad or had affected his head. The bedraggled bunch that we now were, started off towards Lazenby village and the nearest bus stop. It felt great just to be able to rest my feet up whilst we waited for the bus, and shuffling my bum on to the grass verge and taking the weight off my feet, well it felt like bliss. And it was quite a wait too. By the time we saw the 263 bus turn the corner the sky had changed from bright daylight to a warm glowing twilight, dusk had set in. What a vision. That Double Decker bus was something to be seen, all shiny and red and ready to carry our little exhausted bodies home. How comfy the big old seats felt as we plonked ourselves down in them while we waited for the bus to get going and the conductor to come and collect our fares. He must have been up on the top deck when we got on, because the first I saw of him was when he swung off the bottom step and projected himself towards us shouting "fares please".

Our dad reached for the change in his pocket and asked for "One and three halves to Mersey road please." Mersey road being the nearest stop on the 263 route to our house, and was where our mam bumped into Aunty Renate in the Big Move.

"That'll be two and six" the conductor nonchalantly replied as he began to roll the tickets off the little ticket machine strapped over his shoulder. The calm soon robbed from his face as our dad replied in his 'what the blooming heck do you mean' booming voice.

"Did you just ask for two and six? Two and six?" god you could see it sinking in!

"two and six, that's daylight blooming robbery that is" tightwad chocked, the phrase repeated so as to grasp the seriousness of this outrageous request.

I stole a look at our Karen, who was trying her best to hold a look of total nonchalance, I'm not really with this man on her face but failing miserably, and then one at our Gary who was the colour of fresh beetroot, and could see we were all thinking the same, 'please God make us just disappear!'

I watched as all three of us slopped down in our seats, trying to make ourselves invisible and hoping that nobody on the bus would recognised us and god forbid there be any of our school pals there.

"Stop this bus now, we're getting off here!" he continued in his booming voice that reverberated round the whole of the bus, he jumped up out of his seat and started punching the bell with his thumb. The bus came to such an immediate stand still, you just knew the driver must have thought there'd been an accident. All three of us were launched unceremoniously out of our seats along with half the other folks onboard and landed on the floor, from where our dad herded us up the aisle and past all the gawping slack jawed passengers, who were by now being thoroughly entertained by the whole scene unfolding in front of them and off the bus. What came next was the longest walk of my little life, those three miles felt like three thousand, sore feet, sunburned neck and all three of us covered from head to toe in mortification.

Our dad…tightwad had struck again.

Chapter nine

The Icing on the Cake!

Of all the stories that I am recalling in this little book, none is more legendary in the McManus family than the 'Icing on the cake legend/myth'. Retold and retold to us on so many occasions over the years as we were growing up, that it has reached gigantuous proportions. In fact it is no longer just a family legend, but has taken on mythical qualities that far outweigh any of the other inferior in comparison family tales. Not only is it's legendness limitless (now that's a bit of a mouthful to say), but the answer to the question, 'who ate the cream out of the cake?' stayed elusive to me until I reached my early forties and even then was never really made 100% clear. I continually quizzed both of my siblings about the whole escapade, alas they both always seemed to have forgotten any involvement on their part and always managed to change the subject or just shrug it off, hmm typical!
To my mind, the reason for it being such an extraordinary family legend is to do with the fact that me, miss 100% unequalled over the years in naughtiness, little swine that I was, well,….I didn't do it!
A rarity in my childhood/swinehood.
It is a story all future McManus's can learn lessons from, one of these lessons being never to marry into the volatile Gunn family like our dad had done and always, always have your wits about you whatever the situation!
Now I'm not saying our mam was a bad mam, but god, did she have her moments. One minute she was all sweetness and light, thoroughly entertaining and caring mother, but in an instant, without any prior warning or for any

explainable reason, or so it seemed to us, she could turn into a demonic monster with an ear piercing screech and flaying arms for smacking us with. Her uncontrollable anger could just spill out for no apparent reason and god forbid any one of the three of us who just happened to be in the way of it. You never did quite know what was going to tip her over the edge. The most innocuous thing that you had done the day before and gotten away with without any drama unfolding could suddenly make her snap.

With hindsight I can see how stressful her life must have been, what with her having three kids in less than three years, no real support from any family members because they all still lived in Middlesbrough and we had upped sticks and moved to Redcar. Getting to and from places not being easy without any access to a car, and all of this before she even turned twenty two. The only support system around her being the Aunties who lived in our Close and they all had their own day-to-day dramas to deal with. Now-a-days our mam would have been medicated and on the odd occasion she may even have merited being hospitalised.

The day of the cake incident all those years ago started off just like any old day. It was one of those lovely, wistful sunny summer days, which I had decided to spend up at Gypsy woods. Out of the house at the crack of dawn after making myself a jam sandwich wrapped in the greaseproof paper that had previously been the wrapper from a loaf of Mothers Pride bread, (we knew how to recycle in them days) to take with me in my cardigan pocket.

Hours of idling away spent swinging on the big old tarzee, beck jumping, day-dreaming and generally whiling away the blissful day the way only a six year old can.

Traipsing home full of mud after you notice the light turn from day to dusk, exhausted, completely spent and absolutely starving, hoping to make it home without having to run before the sun slipped all the way down. A head full of plans and plots about how to spend my next day's adventure and with absolutely no idea of the horror that lay in wait for me. If I'd had the slightest inkling about what was about to greet me I might have just dawdled the whole way home or even called in at one of the Aunties until hurricane Maureen had blown over.

Now for you to be able to get a good understanding of the enormity of the event, I need to fill you in with a bit of background information, this way you will have a better understanding of the big picture as my story unfolds.

Stephan Firman was our next-door neighbour-but-one, she was Paul and Alison Firman's mam and married to Tony, who had the best motorbike and sidecar you ever had the chance to have a ride on. Paul being one of the lucky kids to get an ace hairdo from Kazza Snippy Fingers earlier on in the year, and, boy oh boy, could Steph bake! Her cakes were renown in the whole of the six Closes, Fanny Cradock eat your blooming heart out, Steph could walk all over you with her amazing repertoire of fabulous cakes. The piece-de-resistance being her chocolate Victoria sponge cake with its delicious jam and butter cream filling topped off with a dusting of icing sugar. My mouth is watering just remembering the soft spongy texture of her scrumptious cakes, which I can honestly say, hand on heart, have never in all my cake eating years (and there have been a lot) been surpassed. And Aunty Steph was a lovely, generous lady who I remember always having a huge smile on her pretty face. Well, she would bake the odd cake to order for her friends or family, and had done just that for our mam because Audrey Heathcock's birthday was coming up and our mam wanted to surprise her friends with a lovely cake. (I think our mam was going to try and pass it off as one of her own, because the week before she had bought the Bero book and had had a go at a couple of the recipes but without very much success. The sly mare!)

On the morning of my jolly jaunt up to Gypsy woods, Steph had popped round with the two tier beauty and had left it in the large, cool pantry which opened up, just off to the left hand side of the kitchen when you stepped in the back door. The pantry was a large dark windowless cupboard with concrete shelves where we stored the groceries, because even in the summer months it stayed good and cool. We even kept the milk in there stood in a bucket of water before we could afford a fridge. She had sat the cake in the centre of the lower shelve which had been covered with orange and brown floral patterned sticky-back-plastic to help keep it wipe cleanable. This shelf being just about perfectly lined up at eye level for us three little ones to get a good view of, and lent itself to irresistible temptation to anyone of us who opened the pantry door. And tempted one of us was, so it turned out.

On my way home from Gypsy woods, I had decided to approached the house via the back garden route, at this was the quickest way in. I don't think we ever really used the front door, in fact I don't remember ever using anyone of our neighbours front door, the backdoor to all of our aunties houses were never locked.

The only time I remember the front door was ever opened was to pick up the glass bottle of milk from the front doorstep, which the milkman had delivered during the early hours of the morning. Bringing the milk in being a job I particularly relished and often volunteered to do because sometimes, if our mam was a bit preoccupies with something in the back kitchen or if she was in the back garden having her first ciggy of the morning and out of eye shot, I could pop my finger through the foil lid that was sealed around the rim of the bottle, guzzle the cream that had settled at the top and blame those blooming greedy birds.

As I stealthily opened the creaking gates at the bottom of the garden, so as not to draw any attention to the late hour I had gotten myself home, I could see all the lights on in the house and could hear the high pitched screeching that could only belong to one person. Demonic mother!!!
I wasn't too perturbed by this as I could see clearly into the living room through the naughty net curtains that hung at the back window. Our Karen was on the receiving end of one of our mam's tirades. She must have been caught getting up to mischief, which wasn't like her, she was usually very well behaved and if she wasn't, well she was usually very good at hiding it.
Also I had been out playing since the sun came up so it was nowt to do with me. How wrong could one little minx be.
I made my way tentatively up the long, thin, single paving stone wide garden path, past the concrete block shed at the bottom of the garden (where we could store our bikes if we ever had the good fortune to get any), and further up past the fuchsia pink Peony roses which grew amazingly well

behind our Karen's little pet cemetery, this being where the corpses of all her not so lucky pets resided, each one of them marked with a little cross made from discarded lolly sticks and a bit of wire tying them together. Until finally creeping my sneaky way past the coal bunker, which was rarely ever full, then with a bit of good fortune, in through the back kitchen door, without being noticed.

Well our mam, with ears like a big black fruit bat must have heard the door as it slowly creaked open, she must have decided she'd had enough of going for our Karen and dropped her out of her clutches. She now made me the new target for whatever had gotten her so unbelievably worked up this time around. She sprinted as fast as an Olympic gold medalist setting a world record from the front room to the kitchen, with such velocity that a vacuum was caused which sucked the door handle clean out of my clenched hands. And there she was, looming over me, totally unraveled, looking like a wild woman of Wonga. She grabbed me by the scruff of my scrawny neck and spun me round to face the open pantry door, with her bare foot she kicked the back door shut behind me.

"Did you do it?" She screamed at me as she pushed me further into the pantry with hands that were shaking uncontrollably with rage. I could feel the air shift from warm to cool the further she shoved me into the cold dark space of the large airless cupboard.

"Do what?" I asked in all innocence, my eyes as wide as saucers in my face, looking up into hers, searching for some sort of idea of what she was talking about. Alas, nothing. I frantically scratched around in my head for a clue as to what she was screaming about.

"Don't you 'do what' with me, you little minx! Look at it! That beautiful cake! The one Aunty Steph baked this very

morning, totally destroyed!" bits of her spit were landing on my face as she vented every ounce of rage onto me.
I positioned myself closer to the cake to get a good hard look, there wasn't any light in the pantry just a bare socket hanging from the ceiling, and it took my eyes a short time to adjust to this and see what all the hallowbaloo was about.

Some little monkey had ran their little monkey fingers between the top and bottom layers of the thick chocolaty soft sponge and scraped all the jam and buttery cream filling out of the middle of that victim of a cake. It sat slightly lob sided on the shelf, tiny pieces of crumbs scattered on the glass plate and there were small fingerprints embedded in the icing sugar on the top. It did look more than slightly forlorn.

Well, a rather enormous sense of injustice entered my precocious little head. How dare our mam, in her demented rage, accuse me of such an atrocious attack on Steph's beautiful cake? How dare she accuse totally innocent me of defiling the work of art that Steph's beautiful cake was.

Okay, in her defence, if I hadn't have left the house at such an ungodly hour on that morning and had known it was going to be sitting there, in the cool dark of the pantry, all day, Well, I have to admit it would have been just a tad too much temptation for me to bare, and I would have been the culprit.

But I had been gone the whole of that summers day and with only a slightly curled up at the corners jam sandwich to keep me company, I'll have you know. I hadn't touched that beautiful cake, so with that in mind, I felt the most amazing sense of innocence wrapping itself around me, which was a completely brand new experience for me to behold.

"Our mam, I can't believe that you would accuse me of such a terrible thing? I've been out of the house all day". This said in my most pathetic, I can't believe you thought it was me voice.

Oh blooming heck, those fluttering eyelashes I'd just used hadn't evoked even the slightest resemblance to the response I had been hoping to get.

Shifting my weight from one foot to another, breathing deeply and closing my eyes I tried to stay calm and rack my brains for a new and much better strategy. Come on girl you can do it!!! I could feel some serious backtracking was most definitely needed as demonic mother man-handled me by my small bony shoulders and swung me round, dizzyingly fast to face her. She had now positioned herself down on one knee, for maximum effect, giving me an up close and personal look at the mania in her bulging red 'possessed by the devil himself' eyes.

I'm thinking, in no uncertain terms here, that I most definitely have just gone and blurted out the wrong thing, as it, honest to God, looked like steam was starting to come out of her ears. My poor little frazzled brain was now going ten to the dozen, I'm going to have to come up with something absolutely blooming beyond amazing if I want to get out of this little scrap fully intact.

"Honest mam, it wasn't me" I'm clutching at teeny tiny straws here, "I've been up at Gypsy woods all day and you know I would never ever in a month of Sundays admit to that unless it was absolutely true".

I stole a glance across the kitchen at my cowering sister, who physically winced when I imparted the last sentence, she was doing the zip sign across her tightly closed lips with one hand and the sign of the cross on her chest with the other as she fixed her eyes fully on to mine, not a very good omen.

I wasn't allowed to go up to the woods by myself, it was miles to far away, main roads had to be crossed, bushes had to be crawled through and there were all sorts of folks and gypsies just dying to pinch me, and steal me away to have as their own…..as if!

"Gypsy woods!" she continued, spitting the words into my face, as I backed off, one gentle ever-so-slow footstep at a time, stealing through the open doorway and into the front room, trying to create a bit of space between my little target of a body and her looming presence without being noticed, all the while eyeballing for an escape route if she decided to pounce.

"Gypsy woods! Gypsy woods!" repeated twice to pound the words into my head so as to make sure I could get the whole seriousness of them.

"How many times have I told you about going up there? Over and over again!!!"

Well, the diversion tactic of admitting to a little crime to escape the penalty of a big one that I had plumed for seemed to have backfired big-style. It didn't take a professor with a Tefal forehead to see I was in serious trouble if I didn't think fast on my size ten feet. She was emphasising each and every syllable of the words she spat in my face with a pokey index finger, prodding her sharp nail into my runty little chest, pushing me further and further past our Karen and into the sparsely furnished front room. She had, by now, backed me up as far as I could possibly go, right up against the fireplace. There was no place left for her to back me into so I stepped up onto the hearth in front of the unlit fire. I twisted my arm and reached my hand out behind me to steady myself so as not to fall into the grate or knock any of the socks and knickers off the fireguard stood in front of it, but lordy lord, this was, by far and away, the worst move of my little soon to be over, cut off in its prime life. As I placed my small dirty hand on the top of the fireplace behind me to stop myself from falling, unbeknownst to me, our mam's last fag, which she had just borrowed from Aunty Joyce next-door was resting there all on it's own-some, without a care in its little inanimate world, and I felt the bum fall out of my scruffy, with holes in the knees, trousers as that fag snapped under the weight of my little fingers!!!!!!!!

The colour drained right out of me and escaped across the room, I knew I was dead meat and my whole life of about five years passed in front of my wide open slightly glazed over green eyes. I held my breath and shut my eyes tightly, curled my hands into balls, causing my fingernails to bite into my palms and waited in horror for her to notice what I had accidentally done. I waited for her to grab me by the throat and with both her hands around my scrawny neck, shake me to my premature death.

I envisaged the funeral procession, I'd have six white horses pulling my glass rose filled carriage, a bit like Snow Whites, through the Closes, every one of the Aunties and their kids would be weeping and wailing. Mam, in handcuffs, would be down on her knees, begging my forgiveness from inside my white coffin.

But, there is a god in heaven above and he loves me, because at that very moment in time, just as I was about to cast our Kaz and Gary in their funeral attire into my daydream, our Gary waltzed in the back kitchen door, without a care in his little world, whistling a little ditty to himself and totally diverted demonic mother's attention away from me.

'Jesus, Mary and Joseph! That was an unbelievable close shave!!!!' I thought as I was brought back down to earth with the bang of the door. I squirreled myself as far away as was humanly possible from the incriminating broken fag, making sure to do this extremely covertly so as not to draw any unwanted attention back in my direction.

I gingerly watched as my sweet and innocent, soon to be dead and carted off in his glass carriage little brother underwent his interrogation from the safe vantage point of the open passage doorway.

Poor little lamb that he was, he had no idea what he had stepped into that evening after what was to him a run of the mill being good as gold type of day. He had the stunned look of a rabbit caught in the head lights of a Morris Minor across his innocent little astounded face, his big blue eyes wide open and glazed over in shock as mam began poking her finger into his chest and accusing him of stealing the cream out of the cake.

Now, here is the quandary I was in for all of my growing up years, I never laid a grubby little finger on Aunty Steph's blooming cake, so in my young eyes I should never ever have been put in the precarious position of being able to snap the borrowed last fag that was ours mam's. So when she backed our Gary up against the fireplace with her proddy finger, with accusations spat into his darling angel like face and noticed it, well, as far as I was concerned, it was too late for him and I just ducked out of view and saved myself. I knew in her maniacal state that our mam would never bother to stop to ask 'who had snapped it?' her last fag, the one she had just begged Joyce

Simmons from next door to lend her, no chance of another until in the morning, she'd have to just light up the little half inch binge end that was still attached to the filter (and she did) the idea of which she just couldn't bare and it sent her over the edge. I knew she needed someone to vent all that pent up rage and frustration on, right here and right now, and he just stood there, right in front of her, looking as soft and scared as Bambi on the ice as the volcano that was Maureen exploded all over him.

Even if we had wanted to, which we both did, there was nothing me or our Karen could have done to save him, so instead our punishment was to watch. And all I can say is it was a good job the fire wasn't on that night or he just might have been chucked on it.

So the next morning when two pairs of scornful eyes looked at me, one pair full of accusations and dismay, the other pair black and blue, I took the only defence tactic a manipulative little minx like me had to attacked them both with and asked the legendary question......

"Well okay, I snapped the fag, but which one of you two greedy fat grunters ate the icing from the middle of that cake!!!!!!!"

Chapter ten

The Best Summer Ever!

When I look back on my early childhood years, I can see that most of my recollections are good ones, and this leads me to believe that the strange and sometimes plain bonkers upbringing that I had played a hefty part in molding the person that I grew up to became today. I like to think that my outlook on life is always to see the positive side in a situation, and if I don't at least have a positive view then I always try to see the funny side.

It's a bit like this, if you squint your eyes half way shut and then look out of them from a sideways angle, the things you see will always look a little less abrasive, if not this, then at least blurred enough for you to be able to laugh at them. I may have blundered through my life in a bit of a blur, but my god, have there been some funny times.

And, okay, trying to remember right back to my first days may have been slightly difficult, but having the props of the stories told to me by our mam over and over again throughout my early years, and the prompts given to me by my sister and brother after quite a few hours yakking on the phone to work with, and okay, I may have used a bit of poetic license and fleshed them out a bit for the entertainment value, (never let the truth get in the way of a good story' is a motto I also follow, this being handed down to me by our mam). I do believe with these tools in hand, I can fill this little book with enough entertaining stories to be able to make it a half decent read.

Taking the time to recall my upbringing and revisiting moments from my childhood has had a rather cathartic effect. It has given me the opportunity to reflect on the simple times, the exciting times, the sad times, times that I have embraced in my life. All of which went on to form the grown person I have become today. I've been given an open opportunity to self-analyze my life. Okay I may be getting a bit deep here, but only because I have found some surprising things out about myself that have truly opened my eyes.

I first decided to write this book for my kids, close family and friends so that after my demise into total memory loss, or if I fall fowl of delusions of grandeur, I'm hoping that's the way I go, (It really is an affliction that people can suffer from, if you take the time to look closely at your friends and family you will recognize a few them with the onset of this condition, and the odd one with the full blown symptoms)

Hopefully by the end of this journey they will have something real to remember me by. But, and I have to be totally one hundred per cent honest with you all here, learning to recognise the fact that this coming Christmas all my family, friends and even the odd acquaintance who it might be useful to butter up, will be getting a copy of this book as a pressie, thus saving me a small fortune in gifts, has revealed to me that I truly am my father's daughter. Tightwad mark 2! The family trait strikes again! I'm on a learning journey about myself, and who knows what all this reminiscing will reveal to me next.

So we find that life is full of surprises, sometimes good, sometimes bad, sometimes just plain odd, but with a squint and a blur usually funny. So I take myself back to what must be by now at least 1968.

Now 1968 is 'modern times' and could be called a growth period in history, far enough after the second world war for people to start feeling prosperous, but close enough for us to still be canny with our money. There were lots of new and exciting technologies to be embraced, for instance the emerging new-fangled gadgets coming out of America, like the Hoover (I actually thought that the contraption that sucked up the bits from your grubby carpets was called a Hoover right up until I was about 15, okay about 30, when some smart arse informed me it was a vacuum cleaner) and the deep freezer, which folks in the Closes either had or coveted if their neighbours had. We had a mini freezer which was housed inside the fridge, positioned at the top, which would, more times than not, fill up with ice, making it get smaller and smaller, but, not to worry, because there was never anything in it to eat anyways!

I clearly recall the fridge always being empty due to the fact that I was continually sticking my head into it to get a look at what might be in there worth eating. Usually nowt but the lard. The reason I did this so often during my day to day life as a youngster sticks in my memory so well due to the feeling of always being starving, morning, noon and night, not just hungry but quite often ravenous. Some of the noises my tummy made could have been mistaken for thunder, the worst noises being the ones that sounded like I had farted, causing mortification as this usually happened in the classroom when everyone was quite. Sometimes I thought my tummy deliberately timed it's grumbles for maximum embarrassment.

I had breakfast, and dinner and tea everyday just like everyone else did, but I can't for the life of me ever remember feeling completely full, I know I was a picky eater and there was no method to force me to eat something I didn't like that our mam didn't try. Take for instance beans, she would hide them in the mash or under my fish fingers or chips but the runny tomato sauce always gave them away, she would try the 'close your eyes open your mouth for a big surprise' technique…as if!

She just couldn't understand how disgusting the texture of them was. I still can't stomach the horrible little orange things, yuk!

The only time that there was an exception to the Always Starving rule was in the best summer ever, I'll get to it in a minute.

I chatted to my sister to find out if the starving feeling was exclusive to me and to get her thoughts on the subject, it turns out she said the same, the feeling of always being hungry was one she grew up with too.

Being brought up in a lower working class family in the 60's might have contributed towards this feeling. Breakfast was mostly a snatched slice of toast or bowl of cornflakes (never Kellogg's, even though the advert on the telly was our mam's favourite and she would sing the catchy little tune all afternoon when she was having a good day, but more likely, some stores own version that tasted like you'd cut the box into small piece and poured your milk over and if you didn't eat them pronto, they went soggy and lifeless and just flopped in your mouth.)

Or more often than not you would go without because you'd laid in bed way to long and didn't have time to have anything. Dinner was usually at school, need I say anymore, the drama that was school dinnertime for a picky eater was sometimes beyond bearable. So the meal you looked forward to for most of the day was your tea. And when your mam was enjoying the new and amazing frozen foods available at this time, that meant fish fingers, chips (every single family in the Closes being the proud owners of a chip pan) and beans most nights. And as I already told you I hated beans.

By all accounts they make you fart, and I had my tummy getting me in enough embarrassing situations on that front so needed no extra input from beans. But I wouldn't know about that anyways, as neither myself or the Queen ever fart due to us being proper ladies.

Our mam's chips were pants, they were either too fat and not cooked in the middle, soggy from her putting to many in at once or burnt to a crisp when she popped out to have a fag and a natter with Aunty Joyce next-door whilst waiting for the tea to be done.

She was a bit of a rubbish cook and I don't think she ever changed the fat in the chip pan, or should I say lard, extra virgin olive oil never infiltrated the Closes until about the eighties.

So all this left on my plate were the fish fingers, and if you were lucky a side dish full of Mothers Pride white bread smeared with good old Stork Margarine. I still love a fish finger sandwich and have noticed of late they are making a bit of a revival on swanky menus.

The time when you were at your most ravenous was after a long day of straining your brain at school, all you wanted to do was to be hustled in the back kitchen door and plonked at the dinner table, where your three fish fingers would be waiting. Alas the mam who lived with us at 32 Rutland Close seemed to have no conception of what her kiddies needed and was usually sat round one of the aunties at teatime, enjoying a fag, a cuppa and a gossip….except not in the summer of 1968 this being the best year ever.

Why? You may ask yourselves, what could be so grand about this particular year, well folks, let me tell you, I need to drag this part out a bit to add to the drama and suspense, 1968 turned out to be the year our mam only decided she needed a bit of extra housekeeping and got herself a part time job. And where do you think she went and got this fantastic job? Oh my good god in heaven who loves us, she only went and got it at Wellford's cake factory, down the Trunk road!

What bliss, not only did our mam not have to cook when she got in from her hard day at the factory, but she got the opportunity to make her three kids adore her with her great big bag of delicious rejects. It was worth being hungry when you got in from your long journey home from school, the anticipation was a joy in itself, knowing that as soon as our mam came in the door we were going to feel full, no, not just full, but stuffed to the gills.

What rejects would she bring home in her bag to surprise us with tonight? And better still what stories would she enchant us with about her day at work in the cake factory. We'd all be sat waiting at the table, eyes fixed on the door, our mam would breeze in, all glowing and full of excitement to show us what was in her bag, looking like our fairy cake godmother.

What would tonight's delicacy be?

The evening of the cakes would begin.

Let's guess. Was it a Victoria sponge that accidentally (wink wink) got creamed with the wrong filling. Nope.

I know, I know, we'd all be shouting as we'd jump up and down in our seats trying to guess. It's a battered Battenberg, that oops, accidentally fell off the conveyor belt. Nope.

I know, I know, Is it five Viennese fingers that got squashed together or five French fancies that got stretched? Well, we'd sit and we'd eat a face full of cakes whilst we guessed how they'd ended up looking so misshaped until we were fit to burst and eagerly listen to the tales our mam told us of how she made some of the cakes too fat or too short or too full of cream just in case there wasn't enough rejects to bring home in her big beautiful bag. We enjoyed every second of stuffing ourselves full of those cakes and listening to the stories of how they came to get there, and even though we all knew in our little hearts it couldn't last forever, (we may have all been young but none of us was stupid), we all had the foresight to see what was coming. Bless her, not our mam who thought she was a super sneaky reject maker, so knowing most good things came to an end, we relished every moment of cake time our mam stole for us.

Alas, her cards were marked, and it was only a matter of time before she got the sack. But we didn't care we loved her to bit's for gifting us with the whole of that beautiful cake filled, tummies full summer.

Chapter eleven

The Christmas Fiasco

I love Christmas, it's my favourite time of year. I can give or take Easter, really it's not much without the Chocolate, and Birthdays, well I'm at an age now where I should be forgetting them, so for me the best celebration of the year by a long shot always had been Christmas.

I make it last the whole year by spending months planning and organising things to get everything right and see that it goes down with military precision.

Shopping for next years gifts in the January sales (tightwad mark II.) Writing my 'present buying and card sending' lists at the back end of August, there's nothing more satisfying that ticking completed tasks off a neatly written list.

The few cards that I do send being written out by September, I recycle cards by asking family members to put an old one up that I sent them years ago, (again tightwad mark II.)

I have every gift bought or made by the end of October, and wrapped by the end of November, the idea being that I just sit back and enjoy all the festivities the season brings during December in a peaceful stress free manner, well, that's what I aim for but it rarely goes one hundred percent to plan.

I know for a fact that I don't get this trait from our mam who couldn't organise the proverbial 'piss up in a brewery' mind you, she was quite good at the trip bus stuff, scrap that, I've just remember the scruffy bed and breakfast with the horrendous nylon sheets and the repeat mystery tour to 'oh no not blooming Harrogate again!'.

Our dad, however, also had a penchant for writing lists, his were written on tiny pieces of paper (so as not to be wasteful, don't you know) and these lists were to be found scattered in his organised chaos manner all over the house. Today's list of things to do, tomorrows list of things to do, this week's list of things to do, the shopping list, but most of all his lists of top tips for the horses he was going to back that day down at the bookies.

So I'm making an assumption here, that these organisational skills I picked up during my youth were from him.

And the list thing, this student has risen above the teacher that was her dad and she has now become the proud owner of books full of ticked off lists. How blooming anal is that! This is a second trait I seemed to have inherited from my list writing, tightwad of a dad, by heck I'm finding loads of stuff out about me whilst writing this little book.

Our mam, give her her dues, did try her best to be organised, she just never seemed to manage to carry it off, she started buying our presents early in the year, but she should have found much better hiding places for them, In my ten years of living with my mam I don't think that I ever got a single surprise on Christmas morning, but I did become an absolute ace at faking it.

"Oh mam just what I always wanted" I would say in my most surprised voice.

"You haven't even opened it yet" often her reply.

Under the ICI towels at the back of the airing cupboard, on top of the wardrobe in a dusty old green suitcase and behind the water tank in the corner of the cobweb filled loft, how way mam, give us a bit more credit than that, any half wit wearing a blind fold could have sniffed them out!

And then there was the Provvy tickets, she paid a small amount of money towards each week, to spread the cost of Christmas and make sure we all got a couple of half decent presents. She'd pay out a couple of bob every week to the collection lady who came round every Thursday teatime, then at the beginning of December she would get a ticket to spend in the local shops, Woollies being her favourite. But most of the high street shops at the time accepted them, due to the fact that most of the mam's at the time had saved up for them too.

Later on she got a job on the Provvy, collecting money from folks in the neighbourhood, she did it for a bit of extra pocket money and bingo money, which she decided she liked earning because that little part time job lasted quite some years, in fact, right up until she decided to become a taxi driver.

Life in the Closes may have denied me some of the finer things in life, but two things you never lacked whilst living there were entertainment and friendship, all the kids played out together after school, the week ends too and if there wasn't any kids out you'd just pop round one of the Aunties houses for a bit, you were always welcome. All the Aunties were funny, and they all enjoyed a good old chinwag and a laugh, it didn't matter that you were only six, they'd sit and natter with you until the cows came home, telling you all about their day and asking you all about your's. Looking after you until your mam came home from collecting the Provvy money in or from an evening at the bingo, which ever.

I get a lovely warm feeling when I remember all of the Aunties, Aunty Steph with her beautiful smile, baking me a Victoria chocolate sponge with butter filling and jam, for my birthday party, because she knew how much I liked them, and Aunty Flossy, with that big old dirty infectious laugh. She would throw her head back with wild abandon whilst enjoying that laugh, mouth wide open revealing that she didn't have a single tooth in her head. And Aunty Mary, whose house was the most cosy place in the world to curl up in and always smelt of cooking and dogs. Not only did these wonderful ladies all enjoy a good natter, they also, at Christmas, enjoyed a good old get together, a bit of a knees up and, of course, a glass or two of the old amber nectar. And all these little thing accumulated to play a role in what turned out to be our McManus Christmas fiasco, not that any of us three little ones minded, but we did end up spoiling the whole of Christmas morning for our mam that year.

I'm not quite sure if it was 1968 or 69, when events unfolded because, to be honest, they all start to blend together as one, but it was one or the other of these years. Now our dad had a job at the ICI plant at Wilton, he worked as a process officer there for nigh on donkies years, always working the shift system. Six til two, the morning shift. Two til ten, the afternoon shift or ten til six, the night shift, depending on his rota. Then, of course, he had to make sure he squeezed in at least two hours in his second home that was the Lakes social club, before his shift or after or both if he was lucky.

On the Christmas Eve of 68/69? he was down on the rota to work the night shift, which he thought would work out just about perfect for him, because he could do his ten til six shift at work, come home afterwards, get a couple of hours kip, get up and dressed, then be off down the club for a couple of hours of snooker and beer and nicely back home in time for Turkey dinner (we always, without fail had dry over cooked Turkey for Christmas, a couple of years on the trot with a cooked plastic bag of giblets still in it). This meant our dad would be out of the house from about seven o'clock on Christmas eve and unless he showed his face for a couple of minutes before the pub opened at eleven the next morning to see us play with our presents, chances are, we wouldn't be seeing him until dinner time.

But this year our mam must just have decided that she was sick to death of sitting in on her tod on Christmas Eve when everyone else seemed to be out and about and enjoying themselves, so she asked our young neighbour Norma Holmes to baby-sit and she was going to have a night out for a change.

I liked Norma loads, when she babysat she would stay over and kip in the bed with me, she didn't seem to mind that I slept like a starfish and didn't clip my ear for wriggling like our Karen always did. In the winter she would keep me lovely and toasty wrapped in her cuddle, the blankets and candlewick that covered the bed in those days not doing anywhere near as good a job at keeping you warm as Norma did, but I wasn't so keen on her getting in with me in 'the best summer ever', all those cake crumbs, Norma please, being in the bed with them dried up scratchy crumbs, well, it just wasn't pleasant!

Christmas Eve was a ritual in itself, all three of us little ones were hyper and for some reason seemed to think staying in the house and pestering our mam would make the day go quicker.

"How many hours to go now mam?" whined by one of us at least every ten minutes or so, can you even begin to imaging trying to keep three wound up, ankle biting, full of anticipation youngsters occupied all day when kiddies telly didn't really get started until about three pm! And of course there was tomorrows dinner for her to get started on, making sure the Turkey was well and truly cooked through or more to the point incinerated, and getting the pudding mix ready and left in the fridge over night for optimum rise ability, and the veg all peeled in advance and left to soak in the pans ready for the electric ring to be turned on underneath the next morning, all this done in advance because mam knew for a fact that she was going to be knackered all the next day due to the fact that her three adorable little kiddies would get her up at stupid-o'clock in the morning having barely been to sleep.

And then we all had to have the 'make sure you are all spruced up for Christmas' bath, the only one in the year none of us minded taking, we didn't care about how cold we were whilst sat in it, or fight over who got the big towel after we got out of it or even minded the battering with the coal tar soap our mam gave us whilst washing our hair, we endured all this with patience and virtue because it meant the clock was ticking on, counting down the minutes to the big day.

After the bath we all got to wear our new nylon nighties that replaced the old 'full of little burns from the sea coal spitting at you' scruffy ones, or in our Gary's case new flannelette pyjamas.

Because it was Christmas, and the house needed to look tidy for Santa coming, all the usual undies hanging of the mantle piece and fireguard would be tidied away.

We'd sit and finish getting dry in front of a big roaring fire getting corn beef marks on our legs from managing to sit so close to it, what with the fireguard not being there.

We'd toast bread on a fork and sing Christmas songs and listen to our mam beavering away in the kitchen.

Sometimes at Christmas, if our dad's shifts lent him to us, he'd stay in and try and entertain us, in a fashion. He' pick us up one at a time, in his big rough workymans hands and rub our now dry hair on the front room ceiling until it became full of static and stood on end, or he'd lift you up to his face, which always seemed to have a half days growth of stubble powdered across it and rub his bristly chin all over your face until you managed to squirm out of his hands and fall on the floor and roll about laughing. He'd give us all a little taste of Baby Cham in an egg cup size glass and we'd sip it whilst holding the glass between our thumb and forefinger with our pinky stuck up in the air, oh how decadent we were. One time he even gave me a bit of Gin to try, I grimaced , tried to hold a 'Yummy, how delicious' look on my face and pretended I liked it, but I thought it tasted like Domestos, (don't ask me how I knew what Domestos tasted like, I was a swine, I just did), funnily enough, even after my first rather bad experience of an attempt to like it, I rather enjoy Gin now, on ice with a smidge of tonic.

I can see now that our dad was trying to knock us all out with that Baby Cham, so we'd go to bed and he could spend some time on his own with our mam, but he was fighting a losing battle, we'd all be happy to be tucked up early if we thought we could get to sleep quicker, but it always took us ages to fall there.

But the night of the Christmas fiasco our dad was long gone to work, our mam had to wait for what must have felt like an age before the coast was clear and we were all asleep and she could start to bring all the parcels down from their rubbish hiding places and wrap them. This

particular year there was quite a few and I knew this because I'd found every single one of them beforehand.
It was going to take her some time to do a half decent job and she knew this had to be done fast because she was going out. Aunty Joyce and Uncle Abbey, next-door, were throwing a party, Abbey being Joyce's husband, and dad to all the Simmond's kids. We all loved Abbey, he introduced me to Sherry when I was about five and it was so much better than Gin, he was a cracking good laugh and our mam said he threw ace parties. So with all the good intentions in the world she wrapped at lightning speed. By about nine o'clock, her arms were aching, she'd been in and out of the loft God knows how many times, and climbed on a chair to reach on top of the wardrobe and the back of the airing cupboard, sweat dripping off her by now, she'd just about ran out of cello tape, never mind though, the job was just about done, all she really needed now was to stick the labels with our names on ready to be placed on the sofa and two arm chairs in the front room so we could sit comfortably and open them in the morning at the God awful time we were sure to be up at.
I was always disappointed when mine weren't on the sofa, that pile always looked the biggest to me and was usually our Gary's, our mam's spoilt favourite!
But time was getting on, and she could hear The Scaffold banging out 'Lily the Pink' from Abbey's record player coming through the paper thin walls that separated our house from next doors, and the hoots of laughter as folks started arriving at the party. Enough was enough, she decided to leave the big pile of parcels in the middle of the floor, she'd make sure she came back early and finish sorting them out properly then.

More important issued needed to be addressed, like what to wear to up stage all the other 'done up like buttered buns' Aunties.

So off she popped to the bathroom, full glamour needed applying before she could go to the Simmond's party.

Well, it must have been some rocking party that Abbey threw that year because the screams of laughter and loud music blasting through the walls woke us all up well before our usual four o'clock Christmas morning start, and it turns out that Norma couldn't baby-sit for us that night after all, as she had a previous engagement she couldn't get out of, most likely her own party to go to, which meant at the last moment she announced that she couldn't look after us. The knock on effect being that our mam was suppose to pop back in every couple of hours to check on us. After all, it was only next-door.

We weren't worried the slightest bit about this little hick-up when we woke up, Norma was fun to be around but no one was going to miss her tonight, there were much more pressing events about to unfold downstairs, parcels to rip into, delights to be found but better than that, chocolates to be devoured. We jumped out of bed, woke our Gary and bundles him out of his bed, for some reason he always had to be woken up at Christmas.

All three of us came tumbling down the stairs shouting out the usual 'has he been yet? Has he been yet?' this being our Christmas war cry that usually warned our mam we were up and if she wanted to see us open our parcels she better get herself out of bed fast, but as soon as we opened the passage door to the front room and stepped foot inside, we all could see he had. Boy, oh boy was that one hell of a pile of presents Father Christmas had left us, thank you, thank you, thank you Santa. And for some strange reason, seeing all the presents in one great big pile in the middle of the room, well, it just made them seem like we had each been given three times as many presents as was usual. Without further ado or even an invite, we all dived in to open them. Not one of us noticing that our mam and dad were both missing from the 'Perfect Christmas morning' scene.

It didn't take us long to work our way through that huge pile of thoughtfully bought for us presents, Our Gary got Barbie and Cindy, our Karen got Lego and painting by numbers and I got six selections boxes, Yes! Six! Get in there! I soon recognised the shape of the boxes and opened them all before the other two got to them. Mine all mine! For us three, starry eyes and still believing in the beautiful myth of Christmas, it was the best one ever, all getting exactly what we wanted. But not so for our poor mam, who had painstakingly bought each gift, tried her darn most to hide them from us and then spent hours lovingly wrapping them.

When I look back now I can really feel for her, I can only imagine the disappointment on her face when she fell back home more than just a little bit sloshed expecting us all to still be in bed only to find her three darling babies hadn't even bothered to wait for her to get home and enjoy watching as they opened all their lovingly bought for them gifts.

Chapter twelve

The Ouija Board

One of the few possessions we treasured whilst growing up in the Closes was our Black and White telly, this being the size of the average portable these days, it may have only had two channels and you had to shift your lazy bum off the sofa to switch it over but it was absolutely mint. We would watch Andy Pandy and the Flower Pot Men and be mesmerised for hours. But then the boring old news with some suited up bloke yakking on about doom and gloom would come on after that and we would all yawn, uncurl ourselves from in front of the fire, where we would be watching with our feet propped up on the fire guard and wander off to play with our friends or our toys, whatever was deemed the more entertaining that day.

We never got to see many of the evening shows or films that were being aired because we were always made to go to bed early to give our mam a much needed break, even though we rarely went straight to sleep unless we had worn ourselves out being extra naughty that day.

Most nights were spent having a good gossip with your sister, whilst you were both tucked under the thick heavy blankets and candlewicks that cover the bed and pinned you down on top of the soft flannelette stripy sheets, but we could often hear our mam and dad laughing together at the comedy shows that were so popular at the time.

And only on very special occasions did we ever get taken to the cinema.

There was only one small remaining cinema in our town, three had been built in the 1930's but the Redcar Regent which had formally been known as the New Pavillion was the only one still standing. It was built right on the seafront, actually it looked like it was right on the beach and it was an experience to go to. Quite often as a teenager I would nick off school and go watch a film there but it could be wild in the winter and you sometimes struggled to hear the film over the noise of the waves.

We may not have been taken there to enjoy a film together as a family very often but we did get dumped there by our mam and dad almost every Saturday morning to watch the Kids special.

It was a grand morning's entertainment, two films were shown with an interval in the middle and if you were lucky enough to afford it, not us, you could buy an ice-lolly or an ice-cream sandwich from the usherette who made her way down the aisle to the front, shining her torch in your face as she went. If you declared that you were having a birthday that week, you got to go up on the stage whilst everyone clapped and you received a goody bag full of sweets. After my third week, some smartarse cottoned on to the fact I'd had three birthdays on the trot and barred me out for a couple of weeks which didn't bode well with our mam, who treasured this time without us.

Even though she loved an evening out at the cinema, she didn't go that often herself because it was dead hard to get a babysitter who was prepared to watch the three of us, (Norma Holmes may have been fab at the job, but she also had an amazing social life, she was after-all gorgeous on the outside as well as on the inside, so had an army of admirers to spend the time fending off).

But when Dennis Wheatley's 'The Devil rides out' came to town, well, our mam, she was determined to go and see it. It was a classic, mega scary, dead true to life and if you came out with dry knickers then you weren't very easily scared. It was right up our daft-as-a- brush mam's street. Well. She came home after watching that film full of it. All her friends had to go see it, it was fab, in fact, she was so impressed, she decided to go all out and have a Ouija board party and evoke the devil himself, right here in Rutland Close!

She waited until our dad was on a night shift, which started at ten o'clock, this meant, with the half hour cycle to get him to work plus the two hours in the Lakes social club having the odd pint and a game of snooker before heading on his way to earn a crust, he would be out of the house by around about 7.30pm, this being thirty minutes after our usual bedtime, even though there was no way we would be asleep at least we were out of the way, thus making the coast clear for the party, perfect.

All of the Aunties were invited of course, and the house was made ship shape, no knickers and socks hanging around drying on the fireguard tonight, the hoover even got put in the understair cupboard out of the way. A good impression was needed to be made.

The feast was prepared and layed out.

Potatoes cut in half were sitting on side plates, covered in foil, all ready and waiting for the silver skin onions, cubes of red cheese and pieces of tinned pineapple chunks on a cocktail stick to be stabbed into them. The dinner plates laden with Tuc and Ritz crackers piled high with Primula cheese or chicken liver pate, all laid out on our mam's pride and joy that was the family sideboard.

There was a runner covering the top of it, but that wasn't for effect more likely to hide the bit where I had carved a king wearing a jaunty little crown in it with a nail file a couple of weeks earlier, that was some blooming good hiding I got for that little piece of beautifully done decoration, I can tell you, our mam never did understand the artist in me.

I think she even pushed the boat out and bought a couple of bottles of Cherry B and Baby Cham to drink. She placed our collection of mis-matched glasses, mostly given to us by our nana, out next to the food. Classy!

I remember lying in my bed and listening to all the banter and laughter coming from downstairs as all the Aunties started to, one by one, arrive bringing with them, more delicious treats to eat and copious amounts of booze.

'Sod it!' I thought as I untangled myself from under the blankets and got myself out of bed, I'm not missing out on this little soiree. I'm pretty sure I'll enjoy a Ouija board party, whatever that blooming heck that was.

So after practicing a couple of goes at my most pathetic face and getting it cock on, I took myself downstairs with the 'I don't feel very well' I think I'm poorly, excuse.'

Our Karen and Gary would have done the exact self-same thing as well, but, if you're not fast, you're last, and I thought of it first!

I opened the door to the front room, trying to look all pathetic and in need of some TLC and took my time to survey the scene that had been set in front of me, expecting to see the most amazing Ouija board in what I was hoping would look like a Victorian parlour.

In my head the board was made from the finest black mahogany (god only knows how I knew what one was supposed to look like, all I can think of is that I must have snuck down stairs one night when something scary was on the telly and our mam, being on her own and having the hebbiegebbies had let me stay up and watch it and keep her company.)

I had a vision of the words YES and NO carved into the centre on the highly polished veneer with the alphabet, in italics, running all around the outside edge, enclosing the two words in a complete circle. Two beautiful cut glass crystal flutes would be upended and stood side by side in the middle of the board ready for fingers to be placed on and shuffled in the direction of the letters.

Instead, disappointment of disappointments, there was a circle of letters, hastily written on pieces of paper with a biro pen, for god sake, how the hell are you going to impress the Devil with that! These letters weren't even thoughtfully cut, instead had been ripped out of a pad and placed in a haphazard circle on our dinner table. Bloody hell mam, don't you have any blooming imagination? You need me here to show you how to inject a bit of penaze into the scene!

Like a 1920's drama queen I tottered into that room with what I thought was an Oscar winning performance of poorly. I should have known not to have bothered, our mam's face said it all, she was having absolutely none of it, so with a smack on the bum and the pokey finger directing me, I was sent back upstairs to my bed where by brother and sister, with baited breath were waiting.

Well, all three of us sat on the floor at the top of the stairs hiding behind the banister, the big candlewick from our Kaz's bed pulled over us for warmth and our elbows propped up on the pillows we had also dragged from all three of our beds. With our ears to the ground and trying our best not to make a single sound we spent most of the night listening to what was, moments of hilarity, moments of hush, and moments of pretended terror. We tried to imagine what was transpiring underneath us, but just before midnight, when me and our Karen could keep our eyes open any longer, our Gary already being asleep on the floor, we shuffled our way into our rooms, tucked our little brother in his bed and then took ourselves back into our beds.

The next day as we all sat down at the table waiting to be served our cardboard cereal, I asked our mam how her party had went, we wanted to hear her tell us in every minute detail what had happened when she and all the Aunties had sat themselves down at the dinner table, placed their fingers on the up ended glass on that hobbled together of an excuse for a Ouija board, and evoked the Devil, but she wasn't very forthcoming and told us to stop being little pests and eat our breakfasts, we were late for school. She had changed the subject way to quickly, the look on her face being one of pretty darn scared.

But, I already knew that she would be.

Our Karen and Gary had both fell fast asleep long before me that night (Our Gary, waking up and sneaking out of his room and in bed with us because after a while he had gotten right into the spirit of things and the terror took hold and said there was something under his bed).

Downstairs, mam must have been well and truly sloshed on glasses of Cherry B or Baby Cham because after all the drinking and jovialities had died down she started to take the whole thing deadly serious.

I'm thinking now, that one or two of the Aunties may have noticed she was a bit worse for wear and had decided to play up to this and have a laugh at her expense, I think they pushed the tumbler round that board and spelling out a spooky message, and it had the right effect, putting the fear of god into her.

They didn't need to try that hard, really, she had already put the be-Jesus up herself before she even sat down at the Ouija board with all the ghost stories they had exchanged. As soon as everyone had gone, she legged it up the stair two at a time, not daring to look behind her and climbed in bed with us lot, all four of us squashed in a single bed.

Mind you, did I say I already knew she'd be scared? That may just have been because the little minx I was, and for full 'scare the pants of our mam effect', I just hadn't been able to resist shouting down the stairs in a quivering voice as she was saying ta-ra to all the Aunties, that I thought I could hear the sound of horses hooves clip clopping on the tiled roof above, and that I could feel them reverberating through the ceiling, and to top it off, the temperature in the bedroom seemed to have dropped a few degrees and for some strange reason I could see my own breath.

I think I had the effect I was after as she was white as a sheet as she galloped up the stairs.

This little trick may also have contributed towards her sleeping with us for the next couple of months whenever our dad was on nights.

That'll teach you to not let me play your Ouija board game with you our mam!!!!

By heck, the kids today don't know what they missed, you just don't get good old fashioned entertainment of that quality these days.

Chapter thirteen

Way Too Much Punishment For The Crime

If I had a penny for every time I was called a swine when I was young, then I'd be dictating these words to my personal secretary, who would be feeding me chocolate Victoria sponge cake, as I lay on my diamond encrusted chaise lounge in the entertainment room of my beautiful big mansion. I would be absolutely minted!

And if I'm being honest, I shall hold both my hands up, and declare, all the people who called me a swine whilst growing up, to be right, I was one.

I once had the title of 'thoroughbred swine' when our mam was going through her trying to be posh phase. First time I heard it, I thought she had called me a 'full of bread swine' and was amazed that she knew it was me who had eaten the best part of a loaf of Mothers Pride that day. How way mam, three fish fingers just aren't going to fill this little empty belly up!

And due to this swineitis that I had, I managed to develop some brilliant defence mechanisms to keep her smacky hands away from me.

a) Check the coast was clear method, then duck in hopefully unnoticed.

b) Send another unsuspecting sibling in front, usually our Gary to gauge the degree of mania mam was in and hopefully manage to sneak in behind without any of the fallout landing on me.

c) Hang back behind the shed until she nips out for a fag and a chat over the fence with a neighbour, she mostly didn't flare up in front of the Aunties and was usually distracted enough for me to duck down under her radar.

d) My most often used tactic being the 'place the blame on someone else' one.

"It was him."

"It was her."

I would always get this in first, as a shield, before the pointy finger could accuse me of whatever swiney thing I had done that day.

Our Kaz and Gary weren't quite as astute at this as me, I remember one time when I was playing football in the box bedroom, whilst the two of them perched on the bed and watched in amazement at my fantastic ball skills. The door was flung open with full force making it bounce back and hit our mam, or hurricane Maureen right in the face, this just served to aggravate her further. Anyone with half a brain cell should have known that it didn't matter what we said, someone, one of us lot, was in for the high jump.

"Who the hell has been bouncing that bloody ball in here?" she screamed at such a high pitch that stray dogs in the local area winced.

"No-one mam, honest" Our Karen used her sweetest most innocent voice to convey this message and placate her.

"You, it was you wasn't it?" she pointed the pokey finger at our Gary.

"No mam, no one's being bouncing a ball in here, honestly" again in a soft melody of a voice to calm her.

Were they both mad! Couldn't they see that there was no soothing her? That hurricane was demanding at least one victim! And there was no chance on God's own earth it was going to be this little lady.

"Well" she screamed full velocity, at least a seven on the richter scale, into my face, "It must have been you, ya little swine?"

What can I say? Desperate times call for desperate measures.

"Honest mam it wasn't me" not enough information to get me off the hook by the demented look in her wild eyes. "It was them two!" I pointed at the slack jawed pair looking like a pair of book ends at either end of the bed, that did the trick…A sharp getaway was now needed if I wanted to avoid the fall out.

The main reason I was always on the defensive was due to the amount of strange and unusual ways our mam could find to punish any one of the three of us with, if she caught us being even the slightest bit naughty.

Take for instance the perfectly innocuous hairbrush with its smooth wooden handle and horse hair bristles, bought for us by Nana Gunn one Christmas (She always got us useful pressies), but placed in our mam's hands whilst brushing our hair it would become a nasty spiky weapon of evil, that she would smack you on the head with if we even dared do the tiniest little wiggle.

"Keep flaming well still!" Four smacks on the head keeping rhythm with her words, then continuing on with the brushing.

"What did I just say! Sit still" Seven smacks on the head with the brush, again to the beat of her words. She'd then yank you head back with the strands of hair still stuck in the brush until you thought your neck would snap.

You can now see another reason why I had a bowl on the head hairdo, it wasn't just so I didn't get the nits, it was also easier to get the hairbrush through and didn't get easily knotted. I could manage to get through a hair brushing sessions without too much wriggling, thus saving me from a full force hairbrush bashing.

Our Karen wasn't quite so lucky, she used to say, if she ever had her fortune told, by one of those tellers who ran their fingers through your hair and read the bumps on your head, then that teller would end up with cramps in their fingers. It would be like a blind man reading brail, 'War and Peace' was how she put it. All this being due to her having lovely long chestnut coloured locks and her inability to sit still whilst having them brushed.

I have been twanged with a flannel on the legs, smacked on the arms with spoons of all descriptions, beaten over the head with a rather swanky handbag Joyce next-door had lent her to go with a dress she was wearing for a night out. Flicked with numerous flicky things, kneed in the nose hard enough to cause a major bleed, okay in her defense, we were both trying to catch a cricket ball at the same time, but any other mam would have let me catch the ball and get the glory. And when I went and ate our Karen's beautiful diamond encrusted tiara she had made her holy communion in, well let's just say the words hose on the Hoover still gives me goose bumps. To this day I have no idea what prompted me to do that. All I can think is that I was in a bit of a mood with our Kaz for looking so angelic and getting all the attention, or I was just plain hungry. My sister didn't get away without the odd battering herself either, most of them not really deserved and definitely not earned. They were for not being able to disquise her distaste when I was getting one. Our mam would clip me for being naughty and then swing round and wipe that look from our Karen's face.

She once got a good lashing round the head with one of her favourite Barbie dolls, the one with the hair that grows, I must admit, that was dead funny to watch and still makes me chuckle when I remember it. I don't know who was the most traumatised, our Kaz or Barbi?

Our mam rarely had to wipe the look off my hard little face, I was so much better at hiding it than my sister. Looking back the weapon of choice our mam took to me that amazed me the most was when I got a good battering, and yes, it wasn't just a simple smack on the bum or clip round the earhole, but a blooming good hiding, it was with a stick of Blackpool rock. Not just any old stick, mind you, but one of those great big ones that came in a stripy cardboard tube with a plastic handle inserted at the top that was suppose to make it look like a walking stick of rock. And yes, I did deserve to be punished, I was, after all, a little swine, but the punishment, I felt, well it seriously out-weighed the crime.

It was a lovely warm spring Saturday, and it must have been in the middle of April, because our Karen, whose birthday is the 5th, had some money. We didn't very often have money so it's something I remember clearly the odd occasion we did. The reason we never ever had any money was because if any of our relatives ever send us some for our birthdays, (Uncle Bill being one of the relatives who often did this) they would send it to our mam in our birthday card to pass on to us, she would let us open the card, but we had to hand over the money inside to her, which she promised to look after for us, and that was that, vanished, never to be seen again.

But, what do you know, this particular year, Uncle Bill must have got the bus from Grangetown all the way through to Redcar to see his niece on her birthday and actually put that card in her very hands, and our Karen, sharp as a tack that she was, must have opened it up out of view of our mam's prying eyes and hidden the cash that was inside it away for later.

She had a plan. She had decided to take me, her only little sister, on a jolly jaunt down to Redcar seafront and have us both a grand day out, a game of prize bingo and a go on the rides that were on the beach. She did this because she was the best big sister any little minx could have and always managed to give me little treats, looking out for me to make sure I was having a happy time. Even after the football incident and the eating of the tiara incident, and me laughing at the battering she got with the Barbi, (can't believe I'm going to admit to this but it makes me smile every time I write that down) she still took care of me, she was, and still is, unbelievably forgiving of me.

Between us, we made a democratic decision not to tell our mam where we were going, due to the fact that we weren't allowed down Redcar sea front on our own, being as we were only six and seven years old and what with all the crazy folks and Gypsies who would try and pinch us.... as if!

So we made up a right cock-and-bull story and told her we were going round to the Sleightholms house, up the way a bit in the next Close, to play with Elaine and Susan, in their back garden, they had a shed full of pigeons to feed and watch and be entertained by. Instead though, we set off on our journey down to the beach.

It wasn't a bad day, weather wise, for April, no rain to speak off, so we sauntered along chatting and giggling, planning our lovely day ahead as we made our way through the Lakes estate. Less than half an hour later we arrived at the beach, taking a detour to pop into the public loo's that were set back on the opposite side of the road to the prom and the beach, right at the very top of the

Westdyke Road, they were underground. We didn't really need to go, but we liked to look up at the wonder that was the square glass tiles above our heads, they let the defused light in and we would be amazed that the people up above couldn't see through those tiles and watch us whilst we had our little wee.

Next stop was the swing boats on the beach. Now if you've never been on a swing boat as a kid then all I can say is, you've missed out big time. They were great fun and exercise at the same time. Two of you had to climb into the boat to maximize the fun, and position yourself facing towards each other, on the wooden built-in benches at each end of it. Hanging in front of you were two thick ropes with a big knot tied at the end and you had to pull downwards with all you're might to get the boat to rock backwards and forwards, the harder you pulled that rope down the faster that little hanging boat would go until you felt like you were flying, good old fashioned, non-electric, entertainment. When we'd had enough of swinging and our arms ached enough from pulling, we took our little selves off to have some chips, without fish as we didn't have that much money, but we did get plenty of scraps* and when we splashed the vinegar over them the whiff that wafted up my nose made a picture pop into my head of our dad enjoying a day sunbathing at the Nab.

We walked along the beach as we gobbled them down. The tide was out and we could just to say see the top of the rocks where our dad sometimes took us crabbing on an early summer morning. We noticed that there was loads of sea coal covering the beach ready to be picked and made a note to tell our dad about this so he could bring us back in a day or two to do a bit of sea coal collecting.**

We enjoyed the clear view out to sea as we counted the ships lined up on the horizon that were waiting in an orderly manner to enter the docks over at Teesport.

When we finished every scrap of deliciousness in our hands, we binned the newspaper our chips had been wrapped in and headed back down the beach towards the delights of the amusement arcades. It turned out that six and seven year olds are not allowed to play bingo without an adult with them, so we had to be content with the arcades.

We changed all our remaining money into pennies and counted them out between the two of us, ruling out the one arm bandits as boring and a bit of hard work, we made our way over to the old favourite that was the Penny shove. Dropping one of our coins in and following which direction it took through the randomly placed obstacles to see if it would land in the optimum space to make a whole load more pennies and the odd prize that balance on top of them, (where they had begun to building up nice and thick towards the lip of the shelf), fall into the metal tray at the bottom of the case. We would take our time to watch who had already exhausted all their pennies on a particular machine and needed to go to the cashier to replenish them and as soon as they went to change shillings into pennies, we would steal into the spot they had just vacated and hopefully win all their money. Sly little cheeky mares that we were.

We must have done pretty well too, because we managed to stay entertained in the amusement arcade all afternoon on just a few bob. But we weren't daft and both of us knew the penny shove always won in the end. My money ran out first, our Karen topped me up a couple of times after that but eventually her money ran out too. Before we left, to head back home, our Karen decided to run her little hands around the inside of the tray that caught the money and the prizes that was positioned about a foot from the base of the machine and was difficult to actually see into, just in case we had missed a stray penny. What do you know, as luck would have it, there was a prize in there! Someone had forgotten to take what turned out to be a small plastic toy, shaped like a book the cover of which was painted red, it was about the size of the average Swan Vesta match box. There was a tiny peephole at the end which looked like the pages, with a magnifying glass lens to place your eye up against at the sleeve edge. If you raised the little plastic book up to the light and looked into it you could read the Lord's Prayer that was printed in tiny writing on the inside, how marvellous! Our Karen could not believe her good luck, it made her day, she said she thought it was given to her as a sign from God, and she was going to have good luck for the whole of the rest of the week.

We marvelled over it all the way home, taking turns to hold it up to the now fading light and squinted to read the wonderful words inside, but by the time we got back to the Closes, the night had drawn in and it was too dark to see anything, our Karen gently tucked it away in her cardigan pocket, she gave it a little stroke for safe keeping, and gave me a contented little smile.

We knew we were in trouble as we opened the gate to our garden, it was really dark by now, the street lights were on but did little to illuminate to back alley that led to our back garden. We knew better than to stay out this late, and we both knew there was a good chance that a price would be paid. We didn't let this take the sparkle of our fab day out, it had been worth it or so we thought as we approached the back kitchen door. Neither of us being the slightest bit prepared for the onslaught that awaited us.

The door handle was barely pushed down in my hand, when with lightning speed it was flung wide open, demonic mother stood in front of us dishevelled, hands waving above her head, her copper coloured hair, that was usually lacquered down, sticking out all over the place, her mascara now smudged beneath her demented looking eyes, mouth wide open ready to scream at us, the vision of which would have usually terrified us both to the bones.

I don't know why but I didn't care that she looked ready to blow a fuse, You know what? I'd had a lovely day out with my sweetheart of a sister and Gods little red prayer book, with his lovely prayer on the inside was going to give us good luck for the whole of the rest of the week, how stupid was I!

The ear piercing screaming started as we were man handled into the kitchen!

"Where the bloody hell have you two been? I've been looking for you everywhere, all the neighbours have been looking for you for hours too. I was just about to go get the police, I thought some crazy folks or Gypsies had pinched the pair of you" on and on and on, not even coming up for air, yak, yak, yak, yak, yak, she went on, but who cares, our little prayer book, safely ensconced in our Karens pocket was like a force-field around us, keeping the words from settling on us, "and Mary Rowlands has just got back from Blackpool and got you both some rock."

Well, my little ears pricked up at this tasty snipit of information, it was after all, a long time since I'd had my chips with scraps on and I was more than a bit peckish. I could just about go a bit of rock.

"WELL, you pair of little swines, Don't just stand there like a pair of dummies, what have you got to say for yourselves?" Then total silence as she leaned in towards us and held us both in her demented gaze.

The words were out of my mouth before my brain had half a change to get itself into first gear.
"OOO, rock, did you say rock? off Mary Rowlands, don't mind if I do , thanks mam." And I held my hands out.
The look on her face conveyed a message that made me nip my wee in and realized there was no going to be saved by the book.
"You cheeky little brass faced swine you! I'll give you your bloody rock alright."
And she did, she broke that rock into a thousand pieces over my cheeky little 'can't keep my big mouth shut in my' head. The limp cardboard it was wrapped in barely holding together as she whacked me again and again, our Karen just stood there frozen in stunned silence, she couldn't even muster up the look of distain that usually earned her a good hiding as well.
Later on, when my lovely big sister joined me in bed, where I already lay bruised and sore under the heavy blankets, having been battered all the way through the kitchen, then the hall and up the stairs, across the landing and in to the bedroom with that rock. She cradled me in her small soft caring arms and helped to pick out the bits of broken rock that were embedded in my face and in my hair. I knew she was sorry that I'd taken the full force of the Walking stick of rock attack that I had gotten from hurricane Maureen, so she stroked my face and shushed away my tears and held me close, but I knew she was also glad that it was her who had found God's little book and

not me, because it did bring her a lucky day, after all, and she was spared.

*Scraps

For all you folk who have never tasted the delicacy that is scraps I will try and describe them to make your mouth water just as mine did when I was a kid stood in the queue at the Chippy. Scraps are the bits of batter that fall off the fish and into the big deep fat fryer during the cooking process, these are then scooped out and placed in a rack where they are left to stand for a minute or two to drain a bit of the excess lard off. If you were hungry and there were some scraps available the waitress would serve them up to you on top of your chips to bulk out your purchase and fill you up, and sometimes when you were really skint and starving you could be cheeky and put on your most pathetic face and flutter your eyelashes at her to see if she would serve you up a bag for free, which you would then slather with salt and vinegar and scoff whilst still piping hot, rarely did they last long enough to get even a sniff at getting cold.

**Seacoaling.

Now some of you folks might not know what sea coaling is, so I'll try my best to explain. As I've already told you we had a coal fire in our house and it was the only method of heating we had. In the back garden we also had a coalbunker for the coal man to deliver the coal into, but as was the norm for a lot of families during this time it was rarely ever full, coal was expensive. Now, living on the coast gave you the advantage of being able to go and collect any sea coal that had deposited itself on the sand, sea coal was a dusting of fine coal that the sea washed up from coal deposits under the water.

We would go with our dad, taking our shovels and would gently scrape the fine coal up, being careful not to collect any of the sand with it, we would collect up as much as our buckets would allow, remembering that we also had to carry it and our heavy shovel all the way home with us. When we got back we would leave it a couple of days to dry out and then wrap it in cones made from newspaper. When we ran out of coal, which was often the case, we would throw a couple of cones of the seacoal on the fire. The upside of this ritual being a nice and toasty warm front room, the down side being, when you sat in front of the fire, sometimes pieces of shell would explode out of the seacoal, through the fireguard and land on your nylon nighty, burning a hole through it and another one in your skin, ouch.

Chapter fourteen

The Ghost of St Cuthbert's

My best friend throughout all my younger years (apart from Ste Simmons of course), was our Karen, my big sister, who was and still is eighteen months older than me. (I have to pop that snipit of information in every now and then, just to poke it up her, when she reads this, what with me being so much younger than her.).

Even though we are both cracking on a bit now, we're still dead close and good friends and see each other nearly every single day or if not then at least chat on the phone. We did loads of crazy stuff together when we were small, we laughed together often, played together often and fought like two little bear cubs with each other regularly. She spent a lot of time looking out for me and when I was about ten and our mam decided enough was enough, she'd had her fill of trying to keep us naughty little ankle biters in check, and upped sticks and left us for good, well, our Karen stepped in, and with our dad brought me and our little brother Gary all the rest of the way up.

Even though she was the best big sister in the world she sometimes was a right little mare! And I know I did some horrible things to her while we were little, like eating her beautiful tiara and all the chocolates that she had gotten for her birthday as a gift from one of the Aunties (yummy Milk Tray, two tiers of delicious soft centred loveliness.) She had hidden them, not very well, under her bed behind her box of painting by numbers, when she had the misfortune to catch the chicken pox that were doing the rounds. Our mam had made her get out of bed and get dressed so she could take her round all the Aunties to have a good gawp at how spotty she was and make her rub up against any of the neighbouring kids who hadn't caught the pox yet.

Meanwhile back at home I had just read an episode of Mini the Minx in the Beano comic that our Gary got every Saturday morning for being good, Mini was my heroine, and I tried to emulate her all through my young years, now there's a great role model for a young minx in training. In this particular episode she had eaten all Dennis's chocolates and replaced them with mud and when he had eaten them he didn't even notice. I thought that was an absolutely brain wave of a plot and decided to try it out on our Kaz, but being a bit brighter than Dennis, she did notice.

I remember one of the horrible things she did back to me rather clearly. (I know she still thinks it's dead funny and brings it up every now and then just to have a little giggle at my expense). I remember it so well because it scared the little pants off me!

Redcar was a small town to be brought up in during the sixties. It has expanded massively since those days, and almost touches the next town up from it, Marske, but back then it was small enough to be able to get to the outskirts of in no time at all, then you met what felt like miles and miles of fields you had to cross before you chanced upon the next houses.

The nearest village just up the way a bit before you got to ICI Wilton where our dad worked, was Kirkleatham, even smaller than Redcar, in fact it was just a tiny little place. It didn't even have any shops that I can remember.

Kirkleatham was made up of, maybe's, a couple of dozen

or so houses, the old peoples retirement homes that used to be the almshouses, a big brick wall enclosed apple orchard (where a horse once kicked me up the bum when I was apple raiding there) and a small really old, but beautiful little church, St Cuthbert's. There was a meandering beck and some woods too, this making it a wonderful place to while away a hot summers day, which is what we often did during the holidays or sometimes on weekends.

The pair of us would set out from our house, via the back door and up the path to the back gate, we'd make our way through the Closes, exiting onto Roseberry Road, where we would cross over near the shops, past Forbouys the sweet shop, where, if we had any money, we'd pop in and buy a quarter of Cop-Cops or Army and Navy tables to enjoy on the journey. We'd then head up Low Farm drive past our school, St Albans, and on to where the posh new houses were being built at the top end of West Dyke road. We'd make sure the coast was clear before hopping over the high wooden fence there and take a short cut through the farmers potato fields being careful not to stand on any of the plants or falling in the ruts the plough had made. Lastly, we'd cut through a little cops of trees, following a well-worn path. Then we would emerge from the trees right in the heart of the little village. We would have to climb over a big old sandstone wall that circles the woods first, our Karen giving me a leg up* and then me giving her a hand, but we were little scallywags and a bit of cutting through woods and climbing walls was all in an average day for the two of us, if it helped to take a few minutes of the journey time. Once we'd jumped down from the wall on to the soft grass verge we were there, on the opposite side of the road from the church.

Now local myth has it that even though St Cuthbert's church is at least three miles from the coast, there was once a smugglers den underneath it, the village had previously housed some rather shady ale houses that had been pulled down in the 1700's by the local lord of the manor, these ale houses were reputed to have been regularly frequented by these so called smugglers. A tunnel had supposedly (don't you just love the word supposedly, it's been getting me out of bother for donkey's years) been dug out all the way from the beach right up close to these ale houses and were somewhere under the church for the smugglers to sneak through and hide all their stolen contraband in. Actually it may not have been a myth, me and our Kaz might just have made that all up in one of our imaginary games or for effect when we were telling our pals about our grand day out up at Kirky.

We would spend hours mooching through that graveyard around the church looking for the entrance to that smugglers den, we would try and shift some of the lids of the sepulchres with all our little might without success, hopeful of finding the lost entrance to the tunnel that would take us to the treasure trove waiting to be found. We would read all the well weathered names on all the headstones looking for one that belonged to Captain Hook or Blackbeard or something that would give us a clue as to where the elusive place was, hoping that if we found this hidden den under the church it would be full of lost treasure and we would be rich beyond our wildest dreams. Hours of our young lives were spent in this manner, it was exciting, not only looking for the treasure but day dreaming about what we would spend it on once we had found it. Mostly sweets and chips, sometimes sweet and chip shops.

If we got bored of reading all the gravestones then we would sometimes climb back on the big old sandstone wall and play 'dead man's falls', where we would fall from the wall in the most exaggerated of fashions, depending on the manner of death we were acting out. Our Karen never just asked me to act out dying in any of the more conventional ways, like being shot or being stabbed, nothing that easy from her, I had to fall off that wall after dying from the plague, after dying from pneumonia and one time after dying from childbirth, how way Kaz, give me a break will you!

On the last day of the summer holidays we decided to give finding that lost treasure one final shot (if we did find it, then surely we wouldn't have to go back to school the next day, we'd be far too busy loading our trucks up with gold doubloons, jewels and treasure), and we checked all the places we might have previously missed. We spent the day searching around the cemetery, each and every gravestone and even the wall around it looking for a secret switch that would open a hidden passage up to us, just like in all the adventure films we watched on Sunday afternoons on our precious telly.

Alas, those crafty smugglers had hidden that den full of treasure far too well and we gave up. But we had enjoyed the warm September afternoon and we ended up taking an interest in the gravestones and the people whose names were carved into them. Some of them had pretty bunches of flowers or plants carefully placed on them and we wondered about the characters of the people who now lay beneath our feet. Before we set back home we came across a grave that had been more than just lovingly tendered. The plot of which had been enclosed by a shallow wall of about 6 inches high filled with shiny green stones, these stones covered the whole surface, I imagine they were there so as to keep down the weeds. Thousands of these beautiful green stones shone in the late afternoon sun and took on the quality of brightly coloured jewels.

Being a bit of a Magpie and never being able to resist anything shiny (I once conned one of my school pals into swapping her brand new fake diamond encrusted bracelet for the wooden toggles off my duffle coat to our mam's despair). I secretly scooped a small handful of these stones up and placed them in my pocket to take home. They looked to me like beautiful emeralds and I could imagine them sitting nicely with all my other little treasures, shiny buttons, old coins, favourite sweetie wrappers that still smelt a bit of the delicious sweet they had been wrapped round, all of these things that I had hidden in a tin under my bed.

I enjoyed sinking my fingers into these lovely stones the whole journey home, enjoying the feel of them as they warmed from my body heat in my pocket as we got on our way.

When we eventually arrived home we were just in time for our tea, after which, even though it wasn't Sunday, we had to endure bath night and the nitty comb. Mam said we had to look scrubbed up and shiny for the first day of school. When we were deemed to be clean enough and nit free we got our nighties on and took ourselves off up to bed early so as not to sleep in for school the next day.

I wasn't at all tired so decided to get my box of treasures out from under the bed, I wanted to have a last look at them and enjoy the pleasure of knowing they were mine all mine, before I went to sleep.

"What you got in your treasure box, is there something new in there?" Our Karen asked from under her bedclothes as she watched me stroking my treasured finds.

"Eh, nothing for nosey parkers!" I replied. They were mine and she should have had the good sense to get her own shiny stones, she was just jealous, I'm not sharing!

"That's not those green stones from the graveyard I hope". Now she's just digging for a response, I'm just going to completely ignore her.

"I hope not, because everyone and their granny knows that if you take stones from graves the spirit of the dead person who was buried under them will rise up out of the ground, and come and take you away in the night!"

My little ears pricked up at this piece of information. It wasn't that long after our mam's Ouija board night and I was still suffering from a bit of the hebbijebbies and this felt a bit like pay-back time for tricking our mam.

"You don't scare me with your stupid made up lies, you horrible mare you!" I braved it out hoping she would recant her words, laugh, and tell me she was pulling my leg, that she was only joking and that I could sleep easily in my bed.

"You'll see, in the dead of night a lady in a long black dress and a long black veil will come and sweep you up with her long skinny arms and you'll never be seen again" she laughed the words at me then jumped off the bed to act out my demise.

"Get lost you! You're just being a mare, and trying to scare me. And all because you didn't have the brains to get any stones yourself," I was hoping a bit of brazenness might help and she'd give in and admit her lie.

"You'll see" was all she said as she got up from the floor, where she was standing over me waving her arms to imitate the black lady, to go and nip on the loo.

I lay there for a minute thinking about what she had said, debating with myself about whether she was having my eyes out or was looking out for me and trying to think of something to say to make her confess, when all of a sudden I heard a big intake of breath.

"Did you see her? Did you see her?" Our Karen stood in the doorway, eyes wide as saucers, mouth dropping open, pointing with a shaky finger to the bottom of my bed.

In our darkened bedroom I hadn't seen anything.

"She was there, honestly, all in black, looking at you, SHE WANTS THEM BACK!!!!!!!" At this she ran and jumped into the bed pulling the covers over her head and curling in a ball under them.

Well, I had to nip my wee in here, because the last thing I wanted was to be pinched out of a wringing wet bed by a lady in black with long skinny arms. Oh my good God in heaven above, I'm doomed! There's a dead woman in a black dress and a black veil at the bottom of my bed who wants her jewels back. I didn't take two seconds to think the situation through, I was out of that bed like a flash tucking my treasure box under my arm for safe keeping, sneaking like a cat burglar down those stairs, my duffle coat minus the toggles over my shoulders and my shoes under my other arm before our Karen realised what I was up to.

I was out of that house at lightning speed because I could see the night falling around me and the last thing I needed was to be up at that graveyard in the pitch black, there was, after all, a woman in black with long skinny arms going to pinch me from my bed if I didn't return her goods…I was doomed, doomed I tell you!

I ran like the wind, speedy Gonzales wouldn't have been able to catch me. Up that garden path, through those Closes, down Low Farm drive, up West dyke road, not once looking back, I didn't dare go across the potato field in case I lost my footing and couldn't finish the journey, would the lady in black see me lying there and come from her grave to sweep me up were I lay?

So I went the long route, past Robin Lockhart's swanky detached dorma-bungalow and on past the Mcpolin's farm, even the agonising stitch in my side, which was killing me, not making me stop for breath.

I was shaking in my shoes when I got to the church, I didn't quite know if it was with fear or the sheer exertion from running, the light mostly gone now, a full moon and sparkly stars replacing the sun in the sky. I apologised out loud to the occupier of the grave I had taken the stones from and did the sign of the cross over my chest, I was never really very religious but I was prepared to try anything if it helped. I took the stones from my tin and carefully replaced them back amongst all the others covering the grave, keeping my eyes glued to the floor so as not to see anything ghostly out of my peripheral vision, hoping and praying she would stay in her grave tonight and not notice what had occurred.

Then back on my way out through the big heavy creaking church gates, then through the silent village, not a soul in sight, happy to see the street lights ahead and praying our mam hadn't moved from in front of the telly and also not notice what had occurred.

I was well and blooming truly exhausted, I can tell you, when I finally made it back from my six mile marathon, and fell back in the house covered in sweat, hair stuck to my head, heart beating fit to burst out of my chest, legs like jelly, past our mam who hadn't moved an inch, there must have been some riveting watch on the telly that night. She never noticed a thing. Not even the squeak of the back door as I opened it, apart from a couple of weeks after the Ouija board party, that door was never locked. Nor if I remember were any of the neighbours backdoors.

Our Karen sat on the top stairs as I wobbled on my shaky legs past her.

"That'll teach you" was all that horrible little mare said with a wicked little smile on her face, as I fell past her and onto my bed....safe!

I got my own back though, and waited until she was asleep and climbed into bed with her during the night, she hated it when I did that, she always said that I slept like a starfish in an exercise class. But there was no way I was sleeping alone, vulnerable and without a decoy. I stayed awake the whole of that night and if that lady in black with the skinny long arms came for me then I would tell her to reach past me to the culprit who took the stones....the mare sleeping next to me! It may have been a big lie but who cares, it's dog eat dog, or every man for themselves growing up in the McManus household!

* A leg up

We've all at some time of other in our little lives been given a leg up, it's when your friend interlocks their fingers to form a solid base with their two hands for you to put your foot in. Once your foot was in place you'd jump up and try and take the weight off your feet and let your friend propel you upwards and over. It was much easier to be the person giving a leg up that a hand down, I can't tell you how many times I fell off that daft wall trying to pull our Kaz over it.

Chapter fifteen

Our Gaz

When, as a child, do you realise that you have a younger sibling? I don't know the answer to this question, all I know is that I always remember my baby brother being there. He's only eleven months younger than me, so when you think about it he almost always was.

He wasn't a big player in my life for the first couple of years, being as he was so well behaved and boring, and he may have been our mam's favourite, but with good reason, until he was about five he was absolutely no bother at all. He looked the part too, what with his thick head of white blond hair, big blue eyes surrounded by long dark lashes and cherubic little rosy chubby cheeks, well, who couldn't help but find him the epitome of sweetness and light. He was a little angel. His nature was so very placid, he would always try to please everyone and make them smile, yawn, yawn, yawn, yawn, yawn, I just thought he was thoroughly, out and out, don't pester me with your cute little come and play with me smile, boring.

Why couldn't I have a more dynamic sibling? One who could entertain you with his jokes, get up to some mischief, you know, have a good old belly laugh with. Turns out all I needed to have done was wait, I don't have the first clue as to what he wished for when he blew the candles out on his Chocolate Victoria sponge birthday cake (thanks again Aunty Steph) when he turned five, maybe's a more scintillating personality, but what do you know, he only went and landed himself one!

He was like a dragonfly emerging from the first dull years of it's life after crawling around in the mud on its stubby caterpillar legs and spreading it's gossamer thin wings to take on the world. Suddenly out of nowhere I had an exciting new playmate, one who was ready to take the bull by the horns and go after a bit of an adventure. When he turned five I got the real brother I had been hoping for, our Gazza.

By now our mam was well and truly outnumbered by her naughty little ankle biters, and the more I write this account and the more stories I recall about being a kid, the more I understand why she up and left us.

We were, looking back, all three of us in our own different ways, little horrors.

Take for instance our Gary, not only did he suddenly emerge with an interesting personality and a sense of adventure, but a small part of me wonders if he also developed a bit of a death wish, the things he got up to! Or maybe's this was down to him having two swiney older sisters who had a head start on him, thus making the competition pretty strong as to which one of the three of us could do the most outrageously naughty things. (I'm pretty sure I won at this, hands down!)

I once thought that he had been struck by a bolt of lightning, I was upstairs playing nicely with my toys, (or more likely sneaking around in the airing cupboard, or on top of the wardrobe or sniffing around in the loft, because it was coming up to Christmas), when I heard the most almighty bang that stopped me in my tracks making me run and see what had caused it. Sat on the floor in the passage with his back up against the wall, where he had been thrown by the force, was Our Gary, and I cross my heart and hope to die if there wasn't smoke coming from the top of his head, his hair was stood on end and he was twitching like he was having some sort of seizure. It turns out this is what you look like when you've been stupid enough to stick a screwdriver into the electric socket on the passage wall and then switch it on.

This was god almighty stupid on two levels, not only could he have died from an electric shock belting through his little body and stopping his heart, but he was also likely to be battered to death by our mam when she tried to plug the Hoover into that socket only to find out it had been tampered with.

What with his pyromania and his affinity with electricity, I'm surprised he made it to his teens and beyond.

One of our favourite games was 'Shockyitis' we would take turns to stand on his bed under the window in the little box bedroom. We would have already removed the light bulb from the socket, which was hanging from the ceiling in the middle of the room. We would reach up and stick our index finger into this socket whilst the other one of us would stand by the light switch just inside the door and rapidly flick it up and down. The feeling this caused was akin to a big old donkey biting your finger off! To this day, I have no idea as to why we did it, neither of us was stupid and we both knew it was a dead dangerous game to play, but we did fall down on the bed in fits of hysterics afterwards, glad to be alive.

And the things we used to slide down those stairs on, hoping to get an exhilarating fast ride, praying we stayed on whatever it was we were using as our vehicle right to the end, hitting every riser of the stairs with your bum and elbows causing no end of bruises, and with a bit of good fortune not getting thrown through the glass window pane that went from floor to ceiling at the bottom of the staircase. Eee the fun we had!

It wasn't really mischief, we were just curious, full of adventure and up for a laugh but with no sense of boundaries.

"Pass me that dart I've dropped, it's just over there near your feet our Sue", how daft was that, I passed it to him alright and he caught it amazingly well, with his knee cap. A clip round the ear for me.

"Ha-ha, I'm going to get in front of you our Sue" this said as we raced down the concrete slope that took you from the first floor of Roseberry square down to the ground. I don't think so matey! As I stuck my leg out in front of him and watched as he rolled all the way to the bottom on his head…bit of a battering for me off our mam for this one, due to him getting seven stitches in his head.

"Grab hold of my legs, our Sue" said as he swung upside down on the monkey climber out the back of Aunty Flossie's house. Did this boy never learn? How many stitches could one small boys head hold? And no good hiding for me this time when he landed on his head once again and couldn't remember what happened. Not only was his head full of scars from all the stitches he'd had but when he came home claiming to have fallen from the top of the Christmas tree, turns out those stitches made room for a concussion too.

Oh, I've just been reminded of one of our favourite things to do, we would wind an elastic band round and around one of our fingers so tightly until it completely stopped the flow of blood, we would watch as the tourniqueted finger slowly turned blue and not take that elastic band off until the pain was unbearable, God only knows why.

Another thing our Gary liked to do, I wasn't quiet so keen on this one so I left him to it, was to catch bees in his hands, he would wait until the bee had landed on the flower of a clover plant that grew in amongst the grass of the back lawn (in fact ninety percent of the lawn was made from clover) , and slowly approach it, calmly cupping his little hands around it and closing them together. Once caught, he would hold it up to his ear and listen to it franticly buzz. He would then go on to tell you how it was okay to do this as everyone knows bees don't sting you because if they did their stinger would be detached from their bodies and they would die. He caught a fair few bees until the day he cupped his little hands around a big bumblebee that wasn't in the least bit bothered about stinging him, due to the fact that bumblebees can sting you as many times as they jolly well like and won't die. "So Mr Clever clogs next time you go spouting off about nature, make sure you get you information right!" I think he was expecting a bit more sympathy than this from me…as if.

I didn't see him catching any more bees after that little learning curve of an episode.

Our Gary turned out to be more fun than I was first expecting, he had a bit of a dark side and was sometimes a bit odd but was dead clever really. My favourite family legend where he took centre stage happened when we were on holiday in Blackpool. So I'll take the time to recall it from start to finish in as much detail as I can remember and make the rest up, because it's a good example of how bonkers being a member of the McManus family could be.

Our Blackpool Holiday

Now I know I've painted a picture of our mam as being a bit of a demon throughout this little book, but she did try her best to be a good mam some of the time, part of the trouble with her was that she aspired to do better and our dad was content with his little lot in life. Better probably isn't the right way to describe what she wanted, looking back I think it was a more exciting life that she craved. Our dad was happy to just go to work, go to the club and come home and go to bed, but our mam wanted to go away and see other places, and enjoy her life a bit more. After a while she gave up hoping our dad would provide her with this and must have decided that the only way she was ever going to get it was if she organised it herself, so she did. We got to go on loads of trips that she went all out to arranged for herself, us three, all the Aunties and their kids too. She would organise seats on coach journeys for day trips away and ever the odd mini weekend break, mostly these outings were during the summer holidays.

For about six years on the trot we went on a day trip that was called a 'Mystery tour', oh how exciting! All three of us wondered what amazing place the driver was taking us to after we had scampered on his big bus and claimed the back seats as ours. The first year we went on one, the bus took us to Harrogate, not great for kids but we still had a nice day out. The second year, we all sat on the back seats of that coach again, spending the whole journey there trying to guess what exotic location we would be visiting this time. "The Cotswolds sounds rather nice." From our Karen, who must have been flicking through the holiday brochures that were lying round the house.

"Don't be daft it'll be Famingoland, you watch" this from both me and our Gary, ever hopeful of a truly fabulous day out.

Well, what do you know, Harrogate again, doh!

By the third year we had decided to give the driver the benefit of the doubt, after all, he wasn't to know that we had already been to Harrogate on our first Mystery tour, so we were still pretty hopeful when we climbed on the bus, but, there's no surprises here, yes, it doesn't take a rocket scientist to guess where we went, it's only sunny old Harrogate again. By the fourth year, when our mam got us ready for the 'mystery tour' we had a fair idea where we were off to.

So when she said she had organised a trip bus to Blackpool for us and all the Aunties, and get this, the Uncles too, well, we were all over the moon with excitement. It was at the back end of September so as to experience the spectacular that was Blackpool Illuminations and we even got a day off school to go, could it get any better? We got kitted out with new clobber, Aunty Cathy, who lived in the house opposite ours was a bit of a seamstress on the side, she made me and our Kaz some matching outfits and our mam got her knitting needles out and knocked up a couple of cardies to go with the new outfits, we were thrilled to bits, well I would have preferred a blue one instead of girly pink if you'd have bothered to ask me, mam.

We sang songs on the bus, all the way there, I think the dads had cracked open the beer even before the journey had begun and were getting in the spirit.

"She'll be coming down the mountain when she comes, he ah"

"What shall we do with a drunken sailor, what shall we do with the drunken sailor erlie in the morning"

Someone even belted out a couple of verses of Tom Jones's 'My, My, My Delilah".

Everyone was getting in the party mood and the good old Tupperware came out full of little snacks, cocktail sausages, baby scotch eggs, and pork pie, one of the Aunties had gone all out and made a party hedgehog, you know cocktail sticks with stuff on that were stabbed in to a spud.

It was brill.

A couple of hours of merriment later and we all spilled off the bus and into the shabby little B and B we were all booked into, even me, at just seven could tell it wasn't a classy joint, the nylon sheets being a number one give away. But who cares, we weren't planning on spending any unnecessary time here, there was far too much to do, after all there was the pleasure beach to visit and the Illuminations to see.

It must have been getting on for tea time when we finished unpacking our stuff so we made our way down to the tacky dining room, with it's jars of dusty plastic flowers and can you believe it, a set of flying ducks on the wall. Years later I spotted the self-same ones on Hilda Ogden's wall in Coronation Street.

The food wasn't up to much either, but I remember our dad tucking into it, as he was known to say, 'We all have to do our moral duty and try and eat the cost of the holiday in food' so he finished off every scrap we left.

"Come on dad, hurry up scoffing, we want to go to the beach and see the sights" we all hollered at him to get a move on. It was the last Weekend in September and we only had a couple of hours of daylight left to see everything. We managed to coax him away from the table before he ate the print from the plate and headed outside to flag a taxi down.

It was a short journey to the beach and I could see our dad's brain ticking over, working out how far it was to walk back and how much money he would save if he managed to get us all to do just that.

First things first, the Rock shop, what a palace, wall to wall Blackpool rock, humbugs in jars, fried egg and chips on a paper plate made from rock, beans on toast made from rock on another paper plate, but what's that?, oh no, it's a corner full of walking sticks of rock, just avoid looking at it kiddo, don't let the memory of it spoil your holiday, my head was starting to ache thinking about it, close your eyes and walk past it.

Next-door was a room where the rock was made, you could watch as they made the words "Blackpool Rock" and then wrap them in more rock and stretch it to make loads of bars of the stuff. Amazing. As you can tell I loved biting in to a stick of hard rock and feeling it cling to my teeth when I was a kid, the pink minty stick, being my favourite.

After the rock shop we moseyed on down to the Tower, then on to the pier, lastly we all enjoyed a bag of chips which we bought with the taxi fare and ate as we walked home.

All in all, it had been a splendid day and we looked forward to the next as we fell, exhausted between those nylon sheets, asleep before our heads hit the pillow.

The next day started good and early, everyone was meeting at breakfast, all the Aunties and Uncles and their kids, the whole lot of us, and we were going to the Pleasure beach, the name of which conjured up all sorts of images in my small head, from a beach made of Blackpool rock to a beach made from chocolate, you can tell I daydreamed a lot about sweets.

After we waited for our dad to finish eating everything in sight (he was, in his defence a war baby) we all gathered outside in the light drizzle that was just clearing up and waited for the mini bus to collect us and drive us to our fabulous day out.

I noticed as we climbed in the bus how dapper everyone looked, our Gaz in his little shorts and trademark stripy t-shirt, me and our Kaz in our matching outfits. Our mam and dad looking the epitome of 1960's chic, our mam with her bee hive do and our dad's Brylcreemed* Elvis quiff, and I must say Joyce Simmons was wearing the trendiest and tightest flared trousers I'd ever laid eyes on. It wasn't to last long.

I would describe the pleasure beach in detail for everyone to enjoy, alas, I can only remember two of the thrilling rides I went on with any clarity, it was after all a long time ago and I was only about seven.

The first being the Log flume, designed to simulate the journey of logs making their way down man made flumes in the Canadian mountains on their way to the saw mill. It had only been open a couple of years and was causing a big splash with all who rode on it, in more ways than one. We ran straight over and joined the queue, when I say we I mean the mams and kids, the dads had all made their way to the boozer.

It was so exciting as we all climbed on board what looked like a massive hollowed out log, our mam positioning herself right at the front,

"If you're not fast you're last" she shouted as we all piled in behind her, I must have been distracted, I'm normally at the front with our mam but somehow ended up sitting at the back with Paul Firman. His mam, Aunty Steph, had somehow managed to bag the seat next to our mam. Now as we set off I was a bit miffed with myself, fancy letting our mam and Aunty Steph get pole position on the Log Flume, I was slipping a bit here and made a mental note not to let it happen again. I mean, even our Gary and Kaz had better seats than me. Or so I thought.

We set off, slow at first as the log carriage chugged along and up a steeply sloping ramp, rather slowly, almost as if it was deliberately taking it's time so as to exaggerate the anticipation of what was to come, we hovered at the top for a moment then, wham! Down that metal track like a bat out of hell, hitting the water at break neck speed. The front of the carriage seeming to separate through the water and sent it all around the log shaped vehicle. Up again, even more slowly this time, our hearts all beating in our chests with excitement, we hovered at the top a bit longer this time then, bam! down again ending with the flume cutting through the water, we all squealed like stuck pigs as we hurtled down the flume. Up and down we went holding our breath and screaming all the way round until the last hump. My giddy good God, was it big, at least twice the size of all the others we had just experienced. That log chugged up even slower, hovered at the top even longer, and then shot us down that flume like a bullet right into the water, but this time the angle must have been slightly different, instead of sending the water around the log, it sent it right in the direction of the front passengers, our mam and Aunty Steph, ha ha! Did they both get their comeuppance for bagging the two front seats. They had got on that ride all dolled up to the nines, with their hair do's, false lashing, twiggy style make up and posh frocks, in an instant it was all replaced by two drowned rats, and the best of it was, I was positioned right behind Aunty Steph (the one who was famous for the fabulous cakes) and she had never in her life been accused of being slim, so not a drop of that water landed on me, I stayed lovely and dry and looked as cute when I got off as when I had stepped on. I couldn't say the same for the grown-ups though. After spending ten minutes in the Ladies Loos as our mam tried to recover her glamour, we all made our way to the Funhouse. Everyone was meeting up there, even the dads who'd had a few beers to drink and were now up for a bit of a laugh.

The place was like a big indoor circus, brightly coloured with loads of rides to enjoy. Right in the middles was the piece-de-resistance, the vertical slide, it was a metal sheet about ten feet wide, the angle of which, for most of your journey, plunged you straight downwards towards a curve near the bottom which shot you across the floor to a safe landing area.

Behind this there was a revolving tube, the idea of this ride being to see if you could travel through the tube, from one side to the other, without losing your footing and falling over, if you fell over, the tube kept turning, taking you with it until you managed to scramble out. It was a hoot watching all the drunken dads fall over inside it and then get rolled about until they fell out of the other side.

"Do you want to come on the vertical slide with me?" I said to our Gary.

"That's okay our Sue, I'm just going to stay here and watch the dads fall around for a bit", this was a tad odd, It might have been funny to watch but it was so much better to be doing. He had his reasons, so it turned out.

"Well I'm off to get in the queue" actually I could see Aunty Joyce was already in the queue so I was off to go push in. We only had to wait a minute or two and then we took the stairs up to the top. It looked dead scary as you peered over the guard rail at the edge down on to the shiny metal slide.

"You go first Suzy," Aunty Joyce said, I couldn't work out if she was being extra nice or she just wanted me to test it first before she exposed herself to it.

"Okay, here I go, whoopee," I shouted as I launched myself off the top and down that slide, it was a bit like having the ground taken out from underneath you, I went down at breakneck speed using my elbows as breaks, I hit the curve close to the bottom which then sent me on the horizontal bit of the slide and I came to a stop at our mam's feet.

It was exhilarating, I was in a bit of a daze as I stood up but still had enough wits about me to recognise that look on mam's face.

""I don't blooming well believe you" she shouted at me. What the heck's up with her, I couldn't possibly have done anything, for goodness sake I've only been on the slide what's wrong with that?

"Look at the state of your brand new cardy! It took me ages to knit and you looked so lovely when we got here, I might have known it wouldn't last."

I could now see what all the fuss was about, where I had used my elbows as breaks on that slide, there were now great big holes in the wool. Oops, I'm in trouble here!

I closed my eyes and waited for the berating to begin, but luckily for me just at that moment, Aunty Joyce had decided to take the plunge and had launched herself down the slide, being bigger that me she travelled with more momentum and almost knocked our mam off her feet.

"Ee, sorry Maureen, I nearly had you there" she smoothed our mam as she got to her feet, "you should try it, it's great fun".

Me and our mam both burst out laughing,

"what's so funny, you two?" Joyce's face was incredulous, she looked confused, but when she'd come down that slide she must have used her bum cheeks as breaks because those lovely trendy new trousers were worn through , revealing her not-so-trendy knickers.

We laughed about it all the way home on the bus, aunty Joyce's posterior wrapped in my now shabby wrecked cardigan.

We had vacated the Pleasure beach early, most of us looking pretty bedraggles from the rides, and the dads were all in need of an afternoon nap to help them sober up before we embarking on the bus ride along the prom to see the Illuminations. It was agreed that everyone would go back to the B and B for a kip, a bit of tea and then we would all feel ready to face round two of the days shenanigans.

The whole McManus family was sharing one big room with two double beds and a single in it, our mam and dad took themselves upstairs but we didn't really want to listen to our dad snore, so the three of us sat ourselves in front of the telly in the lounge area. There wasn't much on it, so we decided to have a laze about, we were really quiet tired ourselves. After a couple of minutes our Gary got up and took himself off outside to have a bit of a run around, what with the weather being so fine, well, that's what he told us. We would normally have joined him, but we couldn't be bothered, so we just lazed around chatting with the other kids whose mams and dads were also upstairs enjoying a snooze or whatever else they liked to call it.

When teatime came we ran upstairs to rouse our mam and dad and our Gary popped his head back in to see what was occurring. We all sat down together for our buffet tea, this should be fun, watching our dad as he tried to work out the best way to pile up the food on his plate so as to get the maximum amount on without dropping a crumb. The greedy boards went up**

After tea we all had about five minutes to freshen up, then straight outside for the taxi to take us to our tour bus so we could enjoy the experience that was Blackpool Illuminations.

Boy, oh boy, was Blackpool entertaining!

We all stood on the front waiting for our ride to arrive, our dad with his best suit on, our mam spruced up again in full glamour, our Karen and Gary smartened up for the excursion and me in my good outfit with my old cardy over it that our mam had had the foresight to pack.

The taxi arrived and the driver got out and started ferrying us all inside (you were allowed to squeeze the whole family in one cab in those days).

"Well hello there again young fella" the driver smiled over to our Gary.

"Fancy picking you up twice in one day!"

What the heck is this strange man on about? Our Gary is a total stranger to him, we don't even live round here, I know, he must have a double.

"Hiya Burt" our Gary smiles back at him.

What the heck, our Gary knows this man, it's all a bit on the odd side is this.

Well, as you can imagine, we all looked like the slack jaw family, gobs wide open in amazement. How could our Gary, all of six years old have a buddy of a taxi driver called Burt?

Well, I did start this story by telling you he could be a bit of a strange fish could our Gary, but he really was a clever little chappy with it.

It turns out he had wanted to pack even more entertainment into his weekend that the rest of us and wasn't wasting an afternoon on the sofa in the lounge. While the rest of us was having a bit of a siesta he had took himself back to the Pleasure beach for a couple of hours more fun.

He'd stood by that revolving tube while the drunk dads rolled about inside it and had collected up all the loose change that had fell out of their pockets, and it must have been quiet an amount because it paid for the two taxis to the pleasure beach and back that he had flagged down plus entrance to the amusements, and according to Burt a pit stop for chips on the way back, I wondered why he hadn't eaten any tea.

So there you have it, Our Gazza, in a nut shell, not so boring after all, a bit of an odd bod, a bit of a law unto himself but nevertheless as entertaining a little brother if ever there was one.

The Illuminations turned out to be pretty good, but the banter on the bus was even better as we quizzed the life out of our funny, little, mischievous brother. I made my second mental note of the holidays to take more notice of what he was up to and I might end up with a pocket full of drunken blokes change too.

*Brylcream

Now I'm pretty sure most folks will know what Brylcream is but just in case I will enlighten you all. Brylcream was the number one men's hair product to keep any stray hairs in place, and had been on the go since 1928, our dad used it every day of his grown up life because he had a mass of black wavy hair that needed taming, whenever he picked me up for a cuddle I could smell the creaminess of his brylcreem over his aftershave, he always wore Old Spice. One of my fondest memories of our dad was him sitting in his scruffy old recliner chair, eating a pot of winkles that he had caught himself, resting his head on the not so soft fabric of the chair because he had sat in that same spot so often the Byrlcreem had infiltrated the fabric and years of build up later had turned it into a lino type material. The Brylcreem had matted the fabric until it felt like leather.

**Greedy boards

Again, I'm just being a bit pedantic here, because most folks will have heard of greedy boards, it's what we do to make our plates and bowls bigger so as to fit more food on, so if for instance you want to make the tiny bowl you've been given in a tightwads restaurant bigger, so that when you visiting the salad bar you can squeeze more salad in, then you would strategically place all the big lettuce leaves around the edge to then cause an over- hang thus giving you a bigger area to fill with the smaller selection of salad foods.

Chapter sixteen

The Chase

I have been racking my brains for the last couple of days to come up with some funny anecdotes about my infant and junior school days, but they seem to be rather illusive to me. I can only think of two reasons for this, the first one being that they were a bit thin on the ground, and the second being that those days were so bad, that I have chosen to block them out. I can't really see it being the second option due to the fact that St Albans was a pretty boring place to go to school, so I'm pluming for the first and assuming it's just a case of not much worth remembering ever going on there.

St Albans was a newly built school when I took my first steps through the big glass doors into year one of the infants, and it looked rather typical of the schools of the time. It was a single story building, moulded from prefabricated sections pieced together and was painted a bright sunny blue. It wasn't built to last (not like that good old Silvercross pram I had spent so much of my time before school in, I'd put good money on that pram still being the gatekeeper of some unsuspecting baby who I imagine at this moment is trying to escape from it's clutches).

My old school has long since being raised to the ground and replaced by a nursing home for our growing aging population.

No more than a stone's throw away from the school on the opposite side of Yew Tree Avenue stood St Albans church, (built around the same time as the school but using the much more sustainable building material that is bricks and mortar, so has managed to stand the test of time. I can see it becoming pretty darn useful for all those funerals that will be taking place shortly when the old codgers in the nursing home start to pop their clogs. Harsh but true.)

And this was the church where we were expected to attend mass every Sunday….as if!
We were way to busy enjoying a day up at the woods or down the beach or digging for worms in next doors garden, to even contemplate giving any of our precious free time up for mass.
Mind you, I must admit, I do remember once regretting not attending a Saturday morning service.
I don't quiet know why, but one year during infant school I decided to join the choir, this was not something I would typically have done because it meant giving up your play time to practise, so all I can think is that there must have been some sort of worthwhile bribe or reward. Anyways, I went to all the rehearsals, learned a fair few of the hymns and belted them out whenever we had to go over the road and attend a class service.
Well, one week we were all asked to attend a church service on a Saturday morning to sing a couple of songs. A wedding was taking place and the bride and groom had asked for the school choir to sing for them. We all agreed to go along and do this, but I knew that I was only paying lip service, there was no way I was going to be giving up my Saturday morning, how way, it's the weekend and the two last places on earth you're going to be finding me were in school or church. So I agreed to go, knowing fine well that I wouldn't. I knew there were plenty of other singers who would be thrilled to be going, so I just figured out that I wouldn't be missed. And I was right, I wasn't.

When I got to school on Monday morning not one single member of that choir asked me where I had been all week end (up to my eyes in muck and fun most likely) so I covertly asked one of the other singers how it all had went. "Aw it was lovely" she said, "we all stood at the front of the church and watched the whole service, the bride looked lovely, I thought the groom was going to cry when he saw her, we all sang our little hearts out when Mr Walnock raised the baton, and the place was heaving, yak, yak, yak, yak, yak"

I started to zone out at this point and was feeling pretty smug for not going.

"Oh yeah, and the happy couple were so pleased with us all for giving up our free time and turning up on a Saturday morning that they gave each and every one of us a big box of Quality Street."

"WHAT! Did you just say? Quality Street?"

"Yep and it was a family size box too!" I could see the glee in her little eyes as she imparted this snippet of information and it took all my little might to control myself and not poke them out! I was gutted. Quality Street? Quality Street, in my little life I'd never had a whole box to myself, and a family size one to boot. If only I'd gone to church (never in my wildest dreams had I thought I'd ever utter those words) I would have been able to scoff a whole family size box of chocs to myself on the way home. Honestly, there's nowt worse that being a kid and feeling like you're the only one who missed out on a treat. It scarred me for life knowing I'd had an opportunity to earn a box of sweets and missed it!

Now when I think back, St Albans wasn't the first school that I attended, or should I say endured as a child, down to the fact that it wasn't quiet finished in the September when I was due to start school.

 I spent a couple of Months at St Mary's infants towards the town end of Mersey road, but there wasn't much worth recorded there either, except maybes the milk.

Who remembers break time when the teacher would come round the class and hand out dinky size portions of milk? With the cream on the top, a foil lid covering it, a straw for you to pop this lid with, and in a glass bottle (this would be unheard of today, as the people that be, seem to think five year olds will take that glass bottle in their incapable hands and drop it on the soft covering on the classroom floor, then jump on it to make sure it smashed into a hundred jagged pieces, they would, of course proceed to sever several arteries in their little bodies during this process, thus dying in a dramatic fashion, I know this probably isn't the reason why kids today don't have milk any more, but I hate how much they miss out because of so many health and safety guidelines, rant over).

And it was endurance during my early years, due to the fact that my first days at school were lonely for me because I didn't know anyone in my class. Even though I had loads of friends in the Closes, I'd lived there since I was a dot so knew all the families and their kids, but these families were all from the protestant religion, and when the youngsters reached school age, they attended the Lakes school or Coatham School, which were the local Protestant infant schools. It turned out, that we were the only Catholic family with kids of school age in Rutland close, so we had to make a whole bunch of new friends to play with during term time.

The first of my really good new friends was Debbie Preston, I had a few hanger-oners who wanted to be in my click but they were insipid and sycophantic (I love that word and have been waiting for ages to use it!), so when Debbie started at St Albans a couple of months after me, well we hit it off just fine. It was good to have a like-minded ally. Our Karen was in the same class as Debbie's big sister, Christine, and they hit it off too, so it was all just dandy.

Alas, for me Debbie's family ended up falling out with the school and the whole lot of them up sticks and moved from St Albans. Debbie's mam only went and enrolled them in Riverside infants next door, which was a bit of a scandal at the time as this was a protestant school. I lost touch with Debbie for a few years, but she turned up at college when we both attended typing classes and we just took up our friendship where we left off.

My stories about my early school days are a bit thin on the ground but there is one that stands head and shoulders above the rest (mostly because it's the only one I remember,) when Debbie and me ran away from school. I'm sure Debbie and I had some good laughs together and got into some scrapes when we were little too, but, like I already said, this is the only big story I remember we shared.

When we decided to run away from school together still sticks in my memory, not that we got far but we did make a cracking attempt at an escape, and I learned an important lesson from it too. When I undertake to do something now, I take just a tad of time beforehand and think every possible scenario through.

I can see why I gravitated towards Debbie all those years ago, she was very much like me, not so much to look at, being blond with pale eyes and very pretty, but she, like me, enjoyed a good chatter, liked clowning about and didn't take life too seriously, plus we both hated school with a vengeance. We were free spirits and would spend our playtimes and lunch breaks plotting our escape. We would do reccies around the playground to see if we could find the optimum vantage point to start our escape from, we would look for hiding places to hooker down in so nobody would find us after the return to class bell had rung. It was all just daydreaming and a bit of fun to plot until the day we got caught cutting across the school field. Now, with it being a brand new school, the field around it, which was there for us to do our games on and to play on in breaks, was only just freshly seeded, so the whole school had been warned against walking or running across it, but some smartarse had dared us to do just that after the end of day bell had rung, so, just for the hell of it, me and Debbie had decided to go for it. We hung back and waited until there wasn't any adults or teachers in sight then set off at full speed across that 100 yard dash that was our school field. It must have been raining for a couple of days before hand as our feet sank into the soft earth and left footprint size indents in the ground which was starting to show the first little shoots of grass. Debbie was light on her feet and started to get ahead of me, I wasn't having any of that, so notched it up another gear and caught her up. We were laughing as we ran, nervous of being caught, but enjoying the whole 'being naughtiness' of it all. When we got to the bottom of the field, we climbed up the three wooden rungs on the fence and jumped down on the other side, landing in a heap, we rolled around on the ground for a bit, giggling to each other, by heck it was grand. Light headed with relief and the excitement we started to catch our breath and regain our composure. We covertly stood up, looking round to see if anyone had seen our little escapade, and agreed that we had manage to fulfil the dare we had been given.

As neither of us could see anyone nearby watching us, we gave a sigh of relief and relaxed, beyond the bravado, we really didn't want to get caught and get into any bother. We set off in opposite direction towards our houses, me to catch up with our Karen and Debbie to catch up with their Christine, and each of us heading back to where, with a bit of luck our home time friends would be waiting to play with us and with a bit more luck my tea would also be waiting, all that running works up an appetite… and I'm blooming starving…again!

So the next morning, without a care in the world, I set out for what I thought was going to be another run-of-the-mill, boring school day at St Albans without an inkling of how the day ahead was going to unfold.

Most school mornings began with all the year groups, both infants and juniors gathering in the main hall in the centre of the school for assembly. We would say our prayers together and listen to any news Mr Conway the head teacher thought we needed to know about the coming day, or any events that were coming up. Awards for the best behaved pupil, the best speller the usual brown nose stuff were given out, he would yak on and on for up to a good twenty minutes. Some mornings, it was all a girl could do to keep from falling asleep. You'd feel your eyes droop, then your head would slowly hang forward until it reached as far as it would go then you would snap up real sharp just before you fell asleep. And I was just in the middle of this routine when my ears pricked up and I was wide awake. Jesus, I even had to nip my wee in I was so shocked! Mr Conway was looking for the culprits, and with the guilt spreading over me like a wave, I was sure his eyes were peering straight into mine. He was looking for the two naughty little kids who had ruined the newly seeded school field by running across it in their 'hobnail boots' was how he described them, leaving a wake of disaster in their path. I could feel the colour drain from my little freckled cheeks as I turned to chance a look at Debbie, whose eyes were popping out of her head, the tension in her face and neck making her look a bit like Deidre Barlow when she does that bonkers thing with her neck.

'Don't draw any attention to yourself girl' my mind was reeling as I scrambled my thoughts together and looked down at my shoes pretending I was wearing the most interesting pair a girl could own instead of the black patent t bar straps that they were, with a big hole in the sole, but okay to wear because our dad had cut a piece of Lino out and glued it to the inside sole.

'Just look nonchalant, let the accusing looks go over your head and keep calm, nobody saw you'. But the doubts were creeping in and filling my little head. Had someone seen us, were we about to be hauled before the whole school and punished, would Debbie grass me in, or better still should I grass her in and save myself?

Mr Conway continued. He was expecting the two little whippersnappers to admit their guilt and take themselves off to his office and hand themselves over, if they did this, then punishment would be a whole lot less painful.....as if! The whole morning after that was wasted, there was no way I was going to be able to concentrate on my work and to make matters worse I had to keep an eye on Debbie across the classroom just in case she decided to make a confession and dob us both in. If she made the slightest move towards the teacher I would jump up and get in there first, 'because if you're not fast you're last!' Playtime just couldn't come quickly enough for me, I needed to hatch a plan, and soon, to get my sorry little botty out of this big old mess that smartarse's bet had gotten me into. And it turned out that Debbie was thinking pretty much the same, as soon as that bell rang she was up out of her seat like a flash and had whisked me off my feet to a quiet corner of the playground where we could come up with a decent plot. Now, I understood that we were both in a bit of bother if we got caught and my way of thinking was to deny everything and play the innocent little darling that I was. I may have only just turned five but I can tell you I'd had loads of practise at that. But Debbie, she had us both trialed by jury, found guilty and hung, drawn and quartered, her terror was tenfold that of mine but it began to seep through to me with the power of osmosis and my neck started to do a Deidre!

Our school days were over!

But Debbie, the little star that she was, came through with the amazing answer to our prayers, "let's just run away!!!" Now this isn't my usual tactic when confronted with a problem, but Debbie's panic was so infectious I'd stopped thinking straight and agreed.

And there it was THE SHIFT!

One minute we were petrified, then next we had a purpose, we had plans and plots to make, terror turned to excitement. Let the games begin.

We only had 15 minutes to get our plan in place because we had both decided dinnertime was when we would make our 'great escape'.

And what a plan it was.

It's quite telling, the episodes in your life that reveal to you the qualities in your friends, Debbie turned out to be one of the most determined girls I ever know, inspirational, the best way to describe her 'if you want it go get it' attitude to life, she was spontaneous and fun, and really beautiful looking. As a woman she's been married three times, each time a step up from the next and the last time I saw her she looked the epitome of sophisticated self-assurance, but then the Preston sisters all had something lovely about them.

I do like to trail off on a bit of a tangent, so let's get back to the story. Where was I? oh yeah, the Plan.

For two little five year olds we managed to put together quite the itinerary.

1)   Have your dinner, we may be in a bit of a situation here but we both realised that if you're going to do the 100 yard dash past Mrs Wella the dinner nanny on gate guard duty then you needed a bit of fuel in your tank and if you were as picky as me it probably wasn't going to be much.

2)   Get one of your pals to distract her away from her position by the gate, she may be a good size 24 and about 60 years old but she was quick on her feet and would have that gate shut in our faces in an instance.

3)   Make sure Mr Wilky the caretaker is well out of the way, this one might be tricky, got it, someone will have to flood the girls loos again, that will keep him occupied for a bit.

It was sorted, what could possibly go wrong? It would be easy to get a couple of our hanger-on-ers on board to help with the grown-ups, we were home free!   Dinnertime couldn't come fast enough for us and with renewed high spirits we skipped back to class flushed with excitement.

So, how did it all go you may ask? Well, swimmingly to start with. Mr Wilky up to his eyes in mopping out the loo's, Mrs Weller busy taking a look at our Karen's supposedly twisted ankle and Debbie and me flying out that gate and down the path like a pair of contestants who were up for the hundred yard gold medal at the Olympics, hearts beating as fast as little birds, adrenalin pumping as break neck speed through our little bodies, the thrill of the adventure giving us wings. It felt like the wind was lifting and carrying us up and away from all we hated about school.

So where did we go wrong? We thought we had come up with the perfect plan, that we had left no stone unturned, that every base was covered, but we had not taking in to account Mr goody-two-shoes Derek McCormack and his pal, who had decided that it was their duty as prefects to chase us and bring us back. Doh.
Mind you we gave them a run for their money, Debbie being the first to be caught, but not before she got right across Lowfarm drive and half way across the field between the school and the shops. I remember stealing a quick look over my shoulder and seeing her being scooped off her feet and tucked under the huge arm of the prefect who's name escapes me, and just behind her was Derek, running for all his might to catch me, his legs may have been eighteen inches longer than mine but I had determination on my side, I could see Roseberry shopping square just a couple of hundred yards up in the distant.

"Come on girl! RUN!!!" I repeated to myself, if I get to the shops I can hide in the ladies loo's and Derek would never come in after me. Alas, Derek's giant legs were not to be outrun and he gathered me up like a little rag doll, tucked me under his arms and carried me, kicking and screaming, all the way back to school. Our fabulous attempt at the 'Great Escape' had been foiled by a pair of clodhopper clad prefects.

It didn't turn out to be all doom and gloom though, when Mr Conway, the nice man that he really was, found out that we had been so scared that we ran away he decided to be lenient with us and we just got a bit of a telling off and made to do lines. 'I must not run over the school field' had to be written 100 times over in my little school book.

Chapter seventeen

The Next Big Move

Sometimes when I look back on my life over the last forty odd years and compare them to today, I get a real sense of longing for times that no longer exist, things that simply never happen anymore in the fast paced world I now live in.

There are so many examples of this that I still remember fondly, like when I was a kid you never had to stand on anyone's door step for any length of time, you knocked, then someone would holler for you to get yourself in and you would open the door and just walk through it, there was never any standing there freezing half to death or getting drowned if it was raining whilst someone searches for the keys, which were never in the door lock. Nobody's doors were ever locked.

Another example being that the whole family would almost always sit down to tea together, except if your dad was at work and if he was then you'd all sit together with your mam. Always at that table where the food might not have been great but there was usually plenty of bread and butter with it to at least try and fill you up. Then after tea you would all sit together in front of the telly for a couple of hours, watching kids programmes, no going up into your bedroom and watching by yourself. The only time you went upstairs in the bad weather was for bed or to use the loo (maybes the odd occasion to look for the Christmas pressies that were hid up there).

Whilst watching telly all three of us would roll around on the rug in front of the fire vying for the warmest spot and propping our feet up on the fireguard to warm our toes or fighting like little kittens just for the hell of it.

Taking a message to one of the Aunties was a regular errand, because no one had a phone, you would get almost all the way there, forget what you had been told to say and have to come all the way back and pay attention this time while your mam told you again. Once you managed to pass the message on, it could take a couple of attempts if you were easily distracted, one of the Aunties would reward you with a custard cream or a toffee.

The freedom that was given to you from your parents was almost limitless, letting you play out unsupervised until all hours, the only prompts you got to make sure you were home before it got late, were either your tummy rumbling or the light fading from the sky. In the summer you had to be a bit vigilant or you could end up missing both your tea and kids telly.
And of course knowing that you had family extending right the way around the whole of the estate you lived on and not just in your house was amazingly reassuring to a small child.
Inevitably, time moves on, often in the name of progress, rarely do things stay the same, and back in the day, the McManus family wasn't immune to this change.
The first ten years of my upbringing may sometimes have been a bit harsh, but there's no denying that those years were also full of love in bountiful amounts, from all kinds of different directions and in an array of different shapes and sizes. The years of my life that followed may have been full to bursting with love too, but never quite so much as when we lived in the Closes.

Like most good things, these years had ran their course, the ones that followed being not bad ones but something got lost in the move from the Closes and the McManus family never did recapture the sense of community we left when we took the next step up on the social ladder and moved to the old Lakes estate.

We were on the up or so we thought, and our mam had secured a swap with a family who lived just off Troutbeck Road, I think she had to bribe them by paying the back rent they owed to the council along with not telling the bailiffs where they had moved to. It was a small price to pay for a much more impressive place to live, and of course the 'brag where we live' factor that came with a swankier address. So we were moving.

A better house was to be had, posher neighbours, (or so we were led to believe), a bigger back garden, a front garden with a wall around it and a gate. It all looked just fine and dandy to our mam, who ended up staying there for all of five minutes before she hopped it.

The day we moved to 17 Windermere Ave being a prime example of the type of lifestyle we had then, that would never in a million years be replicated today, and that day is a tale worthy of telling.

Again it was one of those lovely summer days that seemed to have packed my younger years, not a great day being as it was July and the school holidays were just tantalisingly out of reach but not bad either as you could count down the days on your hands until freedom.

That summer term I had decided it would be a grand idea to learn to play a musical instrument and had been picked by Mr Walnock, the music teacher, to be given lessons on how to play the glockenspiel, I had visions of me on Top of the Pops banging away on the keys and giving Nancy Renate a run for her money in the charts.

For Christmas earlier in the year I had gotten a Rolf Harris Stylaphone as my main parcel and was as pleased as punch, even though it wasn't a surprise, being as I'd found it at the beginning of December, in that scruffy old suitcase on top of our mam's wardrobe, on one of my covert spying operations, but I had managed to pull off an amazing impersonation of shocked delight on the big day because I really was chuffed to bits with getting it. I spent hours trying to learn the little tunes that came with the box. That little electric, stylus operated, new fangled instrument afforded me hours of pleasure, mostly to the irritation of the rest of my family, and causing our mam to regret getting me it in the first place. I enjoyed countless hours of little melodies right up until I dropped it in the bath one Sunday night to my utter horror but to the relief of all the other members of my family who were super happy not to have to listen to the squeaky little noises it produced for a moment longer.

Having it, even for such a short time had inspired me, so I took up lessons with Mr Walnock, to learn how to play the Glockenspiel. I can still see him, sat next to me, trying hard to hide his irritation at my lack of finesse, how infuriating he found it trying to get me to hit those little metal keys with the soft rubber hammer, and to produce a half decent tune, I really wasn't much good at it, but persevere I did, I had an amazing career to forge playing that thing.

A couple of evenings a week Mr Walnock would give up half an hour of his time to try and teach me how to play that instrument, without much success.

Out of all my friends and family I was the only one who was even remotely interested in having a new skill, they were all doomed to be out shone and forever jealous of my new talent, which meant they were all well and truly home and tucked in front of their tellies or playing in the road before I even set out on my journey home, and even though it was a good couple of miles from the school to my back gate there was never any dramas attached to taking that road home alone. You were given this freedom without any folks tutting and accusing your mam of being bad at her job as mother for letting you do this, and I'm pretty sure it never entered our mam's head to feel guilty. I always hurried home, not because I was responsible or even remotely worried about being pinched by gypsies, as if, I was more worried that when I got home our Karen and Gary would have already tucked into the big pile of bread and butter that always accompanied out tea and that there wouldn't be any left for me.

So I took myself on my way, whistling the little tune I was trying to learn on the Glockenspiel all the way. It was less than a half an hours travel to get me home safely through the back door and I was still whistling as I pushed our back garden gate open and looked up the path to our house.

"Hang on a minute!" I thought as I stopped to take in the scene that had unfolded in front of me, "What was all that furniture doing strewn about the back garden?"

A little warning light had started to go off in my head. Something wasn't quite right here.

I took a tentative step towards the house surveying the garden for any items that I might recognise as ours. In my rush to get home had I come through the wrong back gate? It wouldn't be the first time that I had done that, what with all the houses looking the same and me being such a daydreamer. I lifted my head and scanned the garden next to this one, that's definitely the Simmons's next-door. Tuppence was digging another hole in the mud and I could see where me and Ste had picked all our mam's lovely blooms and tried to plant them in the mud at the weekend to make their garden pretty too. They were now lying dead amongst the weeds.

I know, I bet our mam is doing a swap with someone, our sofa for their's, to make a change and cheer up the front room she was always moving stuff round and trying to brighten the place up, Yep, that'll be what it is. I better go in and see what's occurring, there might be something there for me, you never know. I continued down the path, it definitely was our garden, look there's all the little lollypop stick crosses marking the graves in our Karen's pet cemetery under the remains of what were our mam's prized Peonie rose bushes that me and Ste had picked all the heads off. I opened the back-door, my mouth open, ready to shout something about what was going on, but was stopped in my tracks, the words were snatched from me and I stood there slack jawed.

As I looked around that kitchen that had been a part of my life since I could remember, there was nothing in it that I recognised.

There were strangers, sat at a strange kitchen table, drinking tea out of strange cups, even the cigarettes they were smoking smelt different to our mam's. What the heck? And more to the point, where's my family? They may get on my nerves a bit but they were mine and I wanted them back! I could feel the tide of panic sweeping over me at the thought of them gone, I felt like I'd been sucked into a dream and needed to wake up, I was in a strange house with people I didn't know, smoking fags that weren't our mam's, pretending to be my folks.

It was like the flaming twilight zone in that kitchen, I needed to beat a hasty retreat and give my woozy head a big old shake, so before a single one of them there strangers, whom, I must say looked just as perplexed by my entrance as I did at them being there, had a chance to utter a word, I legged it! Straight back out that door, I needed something familiar for me to be able to get my bearing, I was reeling. Without a further thought for the damage I would do to myself I took the shortest route to Aunty Joyce's, no going back up that path for me, I just propelled myself straight over the wire mesh fence that separated their garden from ours. I got caught a bit on the top and toppled head first over it. I rolled around for a second or two on the bit of concrete path that I had landed on feeling dazed as Tuppence tried to lick the freckles from my face, then I heard the sweetest melody of a voice. "What the flipping heck are you doing rolling round in the dirt, you silly little scally! Get up before you roll in that dog poo right next to you".

Aunty Joyce, you haven't been sucked into another vortex and replaced with a new family. Relief flooded my every pore and I started to calm down enough to notice it might be a tad late to worry about the poo thing!

She rubbed her hands on the apron she was wearing and pulled me to my feet, took me inside, gave me a little wipe with the dishcloth and made me a cup of hot sweet tea then handed it to me in a well-used familiar mug. I plonked my bum down on the battered chair in front of the table and looked down and recognised all the dents, marks and ink stains that covered it, then poked my head in the front room where I had played a hundred times before, everything being familiar to me. I took in all that surrounded me, Joyce's well-worn curtains pinned to the window in one corner where they had been pulled or fallen down, the floral wallpaper, peeled in part from the wall by naughty little fingers during an afternoon with nowt better to do, the half circle of a rug in front of the fire, chewed over the years by countless Tuppences and blackened and burned by sea coal spittings. The battered telly, in the corner with the little black aerial cello taped to the top of it for better reception. It felt like heaven to me.

I listened for a while as Aunty Joyce told me off.

"You're such a daydreamer you are Suzi," she looked scornfully at me, "if your mam told you once, she told you a hundred times that you were all moving house today and to not go to music lessons, but did you listen? As per usual, no!"

mmmm, something she was saying was ringing a bell with me now, and Aunty Joyce was dead right, I could feel myself zoning out right this second, rather than pay attention to the telling off I was being given, I could see a blue bottle on the table in front of me, it was stuck on it's back and was buzzing round in a circle frantically trying to right itself, it was much more interesting than listening to Aunty Joyce tell me off.

"See you're doing it again!" she slapped her hand hard on the table to get my attention back.

"Here's you new address" she handed me a piece of paper, "get yourself off to your new place when you've finished your tea!"

And there you have it, a prime example of the different world I was brought up in compared to that my kids were brought up in and the kids today will be brought up in, who would ever let a nine year old come home from school to find their family had moved? Leave a note with a neighbour with the new address on? And then expect them to find their own way there?

Once I knew what had occurred I was fine, okay I had no idea where 17 Windermere Avenue was, but there was no way on god's earth I was going to ask Aunty Joyce and have her lecture me on not paying attention again, I'd find it, after all how hard could it be?

Actually it turned out to be a hell of a lot harder than I had thought, first off, it wasn't in the Closes, secondly I wasn't that familiar with the old Lakes as most of my adventures up to Gypsy woods had taken me in the opposite directions so it took me a couple of wrong turns before I kind of fell upon it, by which time I was dying from utter starvation and it had started to get dark, but no blooming search party was sent out for me. I ask you, now-a-days you just wouldn't? And to top it off and make my day even worse, everyone had been so busy helping with the unpacking and our mam didn't have time to even think about starting to cook, that they had all gone and bought a chippy tea from the fish shop at Roseberry square, which I missed, our mam not even saving me the skin off her fish which is the only bit we usually got to go with the chips and scraps. I was sent straight to bed after having a bowl of cardboard cornflakes for being a little day dreaming minx who never paid attention.

Chapter Eighteen

Is Your Dad's Name Really Eugene?

So a whole new chapter began in my life. In a whole new address, 17 Windermere Avenue, and a door closed on an episode that was never to return, so I think it might be appropriate to document this, possibly my favourite story, and then make it my final one.

My young life was changing at a dramatic rate and the child I had been was emerging into the teenager I was to become and that series of my life is a whole other book in itself.

17 Windermere Avenue, the address I was to live in until I married and moved to South Africa (book three) turned out to be less swanky than it first appeared, or maybe when the McManus family moved in, we lowered the tone of the area just a bit. There was a whole set of new neighbours to familiarize ourselves with, and a whole bunch of new friends to be made. That lovely sense of family surrounding me, that I had experienced in the Closes was gone and was going to be sorely missed.

The little trooper that I was didn't spend too much time dwelling on this and took the bull by the horns to find a new niche to snuggle into.

A challenge is always something worth trying to win.

Step 1.

Check out who lived nextdoor.

Previously this had been an essential part of my existence, but in my new home, without our mam (she only stayed for the first summer), it turned out to be a lot less important that I thought it would be.

So they were checked out. Flipping heck they must be posh! Both the Devers and the Catchpole families locked their doors. It had never been known before, blimey, they must have stuff worth nicking. I can't see there being much chance of me going round and sitting in their kitchens for a bit of a gossip and a cuppa. Oh well, never mind.

Step 2.

Find myself a new bessa friend.

Ste Simmonds may well have been a fab bessa bud but after he had his 3rd thumb removed and I'd heard all his jokes one time too many, what can I say, his sparkle dulled. Fickle of me, I know, but hey ho that's the way it goes sometimes.

There were, in Windermere Avenue and the surrounding streets a fair few candidates for the job that was up for grabs. First off, Annette and Caroline Wharf from the corner of Thirlmere, I could see their house out of my bedroom window, less that 50 yards away, easy access, good start. Their dad had a car. Bonus, I might get taken on a couple of trips with them. It was looking good, so I decided to give them a try and knock about with them for a couple of days. But after a day or two they had to be ruled out, a bit too snooty for my taste, the final straw being when I was given a bite of Caroline's cheese sandwich, which some idiot had only gone and put apple in with. It took all my reserve not to spit it out there and then on their posh rug. What the flaming hech was that all about, ruining a perfectly good cheese sandwich with apple, I ask you.

Next were the Brooks girls, Julie and Caroline, three doors up on our side of the street, both were nice enough girls, but there family was huge. I lost count of all the kids names and knew I'd never remember them all, who needs that much pressure? So that was two more ruled out, I was beginning to despair about ever finding my new best friend. What if the whole move thing was going to deny me this essential part of my life? Was I doomed to be bestfriendless forever? No way! I'm going to have to persevere, even if it takes some time. I needn't have been too concerned after all, as God smiled at me before I even thought about giving up, because there, right across the road from me, even closer than the Wharfs house. What do you know? There she was, all shiny and blond, my new best friend, Erica, even her name seemed perfect.

Now, there was here, a small problem, Erica already had a best friend in the shape of Stuart Harper, but Stuart made me look like the angle Gabrielle, he could be more than just a little wild, but more than a little charismatic too. Not only did he teach me and Erica to smoke, but cigars! I kid you not!

And I think I may have come along at just about the right time in Enid's eyes (Enid being Erica's mam) as she had just about had her fill of Stuart Harper. I think the egg throwing incident* tipping her over the edge.

 And it was a pretty easy transition once Stuart had been given his marching orders from Enid, I has Erica all to myself that whole summer before school. Boy oh boy what a summer it turned out to be, the big event of which was finding out my dad's name was Eugene.

I imagine you are thinking that I must be a bit slow here, getting all the way to nearly ten years old and not knowing my dad's Christian name, and I know I wasn't much good at paying attention as a kid but to be honest nobody ever really used it. He was Dad to us three little ones and everyone else just called him Mac, even our mam called him Mac, short for McManus, really, that doesn't take a lot of deduction.

Okay if I'd ever bothered to think about it even our Nana, who was a bit strange, (she lived with us for a bit in Windermere Ave, and liked to sit in front of the fire with her skirt pulled up and her bloomers showing until she got cornbeef legs)** Even she wouldn't have named her middle child Mac McManus, mouthful that it was. I never did bother to think about it, and I dare say, stranger names have been given and I actually know a few.

So the eventful day began to unfold, and it was an absolute corker, glorious sunshine and the icing on the cake…..no school, could a day be more perfect?

After ten minutes of sitting in Erica's front room chatting with Enid whilst Erica said she was still getting ready, (more likely hanging out the bedroom window having a sneaky first fag) we heading to the phone box on the corner of Lucerne road, let's start the day off with one of our favourite pass-times, crank phone calls. What a laugh, we would throw open the huge phone book to a random page and run our finger down the names until we found one we thought was funny enough to ring.

"Hello is this Mister Butcher's number?" we would sweetly ask.

"Why, yes young lady, what can I do for you this lovely day?"

"You can wrap me up a couple of chops and throw a ham shank it for good measure!" then screams of laughter as we slammed the receiver down.

"Hello, is this the Black household?" Again, said in the most innocent of voices.

"It is indeed young lady."

"Well, pop ten bob in the meter and brighten the place up, stingy!"

You can see how this could seem hilarious to two little nine year old scally's who enjoyed getting up to a bit of mischief. Kids today, sat in front of their x boxes, they just don't have a clue.

Alas, we only had a few pennies between us so the fun ran out rather more quickly than we would have liked. Never mind, on a delicious day like today there's sure to be something around the corner to entertain us, so we set out walking back to our street. If nothing else occured we could always get the marbles out and have a game or two. But as luck would have it just as we turned onto our street we clapped eyes on Mr Brown, my next-door neighbor-but-one stomping down the path towards us, his face was the picture of thunder, steam looked like it was coming out of his ears! Something had definitely rattled his cage this morning. I nudged Erica to see if she had spotted him, she had of course, there was no avoiding seeing him, he was a man on a mission.

We stopped in our tracks, to watch in which direction he was heading, we could see that things of interest were about to unfold. Hey up! He just opened the shared gate that took you to either our front door or the Dever's. Let's see, oh my, he's only going to our front door, my oh my, he's only proceeded to batter on it with his tightly curled fist.

I looked at Erica and she looked back at me, beaming smiles on our faces. Let's just take the weight off our feet, sit ourselves down on the front wall of the garden and enjoy the scene about to unfold.

We waiting to see who would open the door knowing that, whoever it was, they would be in for one heck of a berating. Mister Brown was knocking so hard it was a miracle he didn't split his knuckles down to the bone. The door itself must have been made of pretty strong stuff not to cave under the battering.

We didn't have to wait long to see it be flung open. Oh my, I hope Mister Brown is ready for this, because demonic mother had only gone and turned up.

"What the bloody hell do you think you are playing at, Mac's sleeping upstairs, after his nightshift!"

"Never mind that Woman!" he yelled back in her face. Oh my, did this stupid man have any idea who he was talking to? Who he was calling 'woman' in such a derogatory tone? Gossamer thin ice was being walked on here.

I turned to Erica, who may have only been introduced to our mam on one or two occasions over the last month or so, but even she in her nearly 10 years of wisdom knew sparks were about to fly. She knew nobody in their right mind would address Maureen McManus as 'Woman', not if they wanted to survive to tell the tale. A smirk travelled across her pretty little face, my, my, my, this was, after all, going to be quiet an entertaining day.

Mister Brown drew in a long deep breath, he had things he needed to get off his chest, things he needed to express, to this 'woman', this 'bane of his life' family who had lowered the tone of this respectable street when they had moved in.

The rant began, and to be fair, Mister Brown did have a good point to make, the problem was he had gone around in the wrong way to get this point across and it was going to have consequences.

I think now is probably a good time to set the scene as to why he was so infuriated.

After the trauma of missing out on my first day in our new house, the whole family, including me got stuck into making the place look like a family home, our dad did the garden and our mam sorted the house, us three little ones helped as much as we could and for all our hard work we were rewarded with a family pet, a beautiful, albino rabbit, Hopity.

Hopity came with a nice roomy cage and a large run for him to get some exercise, but he must have spent time looking through the back window of the house on a Sunday afternoon and watched the classic Steve McQueen in the Great Escape, or maybes he'd watched those crafty prisoners of war in Colditz, because all that Albino bunny ever seemed to be doing was hatching plots to escape, or escaping.

He wasn't a big fan of shop bought rabbit food, I think he preferred organic, because every time he escaped he would ignore the Dever's lush grass and opt for the home grown goodies in the Brown's back garden, Mister Brown being a war baby who was still 'digging for victory'.

That rabbit probably only weighed 6 – 8 pounds wringing wet, but had managed to scoff just about every ounce of green in the allotment size garden of Mister Brown. On numerous occasions he had asked our mam to make sure the little blighter didn't get out, and give her her dues she had tried everything possible to Keep that 'Harry Houdini' of a rabbit in his cage but to no avail.

So here he was, Mister Brown, having caught Hopity Houdini in his garden this very morning. Demolishing his very last brussel sprouts after already obliterating his crops of carrots, peas and cabbage, venting his well-deserved anger to this 'woman' who must have looked like she hadn't cared enough to try and stop the bobtailed burglar escaping. We watched as our mam backed down, she understood he had a good reason to be so angry and we could see her own anger was evaporating with each and every word he spat at her, right up until he stepped over the invisible 'don't you dare blooming well judge me' line. He should have just stuck with the gripe he had about the rabbit, but oh no, this stupid man had taken our mam's failing aggression as an Achille's heal and had decided to get some other stuff off his chest while he was at it. He took the opportunity to go off on a tangent about what a bad mother she was, leaving her unruly ankle biters unattended every evening to go off and play bingo. Not that it was any of his business but she was actually off on her Provvy round collecting money from folk to put away towards the cost of Christmas.

He ended his little tirade with words that surely must have resonated in his head for quite a few years to come.

"And what have you got to say for yourself woman?"

We waited, Erica drawing in a giant breath, both sets of our eye's fixed on our mam's face, surely Mister Brown could see that a giant thunder clap was about to hit him, surely he could see the face of a woman about to completely lose it, surely he wasn't that daft to stand there and wait for a reply. It was all there on her face, right in front of him.

"Go on mam, you tell him!"

Only said in my head so as not to attract any unwanted attention.

And then it was out, the word, just one, screamed from her mouth like a banshees wail, one word, hypnotic, like the sirens song calling

"EUUUUUUUGENEEEEEEE"

In my little life I had never seen anything move so fast, he must have jumped out of bed whilst he was still asleep and sprinted from the bedroom, our dad, in his white string vest and baggy Y-front undies descended the stairs two at a time, his right arm held out straight in front of him like a battering ram. He wasn't stopping for any explanation, the banshee wail had summoned him from his slumber and he had a 'woman' to protect. I remember hearing the sound first as dads fist struck Mister Brown on the jaw where he stood transfixed by the flash of white that came towards him. Our mam having the good sense to dodge to out of the way in plenty of time, because she knew what was coming.

The whole scene played itself out in slow motion before my eyes. Watching the grit of dad's teeth as he put all of his weight behind that one punch. The reverberation of the flesh on his arm as it struck. Mister Brown's feet leaving the ground as he was raised in the air by the force. The force that also threw his head back when his jaw slammed shut against the blow. He must have been launched at least six foot through the air before landing at mine and Erica's feet. Out cold.

I turned to look at her, Erica, hopefully my new best pal, expecting horror on her face, waiting for her to ask "What the bloody hell sort of a family are you?" Waiting for her to make a sharp exit. Instead she nonchalantly turned to me and smiled

"I take it you dad's name is Eugene then."

*Cornbeef legs
For all those folks who don't know what cornbeef legs are,
an explanation here is given. When we were kids the only
heating in the house was the coal fire, so quite often if you
had come from outside on a cold evening the first place
you positioned yourself was right in front of the fire. Now
if you lifted your skirt up to warm your bum, which even
our mam was prone to do, the nearest part of your body to
the flames is your legs, and as you warmed up, the blood
would course through your veins, making them stand out
under your skin a purplish-red colour that had the look of
cornbeef. Our nana spent the whole day sat in front of the
fire, consequently her legs always looked like two tins of
the meaty food stuff.

**The Egg Throwing event.

The egg throwing episode may not be from my history but
Erica told me this story so many times, bigging it up with
every telling, so much so, that I started to believe I was a
spectator who witnessed the whole event. And it is dead
funny, so I'll let you have my version.
Stuart Harper's house was on Thirlmere Avenue, which
opened up on the opposite side of the road from my house.
It curved round quite sharply towards the right, positioning
Erica's back garden directly at the bottom of Stuart's. A
small wooden fence all that separated the two. And
Lenny's (that's Erica's dad) shed stood with its back up
against Stuart's mam's garage with only a short pathway
stopping them from touching.
Now, it was never made clear to me where all the trays of
eggs came from, but there were, by all rights a lot, and I

was never privy as to why Erica did exactly what Stuart told her, all I could think was he had something on her and it must have been big! And in all our 'growing up together' years that followed Erica never told me exactly what it was that made her do it. She had her reasons, so I just took it that they got up to something naughty when they were playing Doctors in Stuart's mam's garage. He even had an operating table and surgical tools set up in there and I felt happy that I got out alive the one time I ventured in.

Any ways, back to the story, it was summer, (well there's a surprise) and a light breeze had risen and had begun to blow a cooling whisper across the gardens. Enid, ever the perfect little housewife and mother, (everyone who knew her adored her) had a wash load of sheets waiting to be dried, so she took the opportunity the wind had afforded her to give them that lush outside dried smell you only get with line dried sheets. The washing line was fastened to the back wall of the house and ran the whole length of the garden down to the side of Lenny's shed, and was long enough to accommodate drying a good half a dozen sheets, when propped up high in the middle. So out Enid pops into the delicious sunshine, hauling with her a large wicker laundry basket full to the brim with damp neatly folded sheets, beaming with house wife merriment she began to peg them out one at a time, five pegs per sheet for optimum breeze catching. She had almost fastened the last stripy flannelette double on the line when the first egg was unceremoniously launched. It landed, not on the sheets, but with a smack on the back wall of the house.

At first Enid was confused, she could see the egg with its mixed white, yolk and shell as it slowly slid down the bricks, but couldn't for the life of her think where it had come from. She even contemplated the fact that a big bird had flown overhead and it had fell out of its bum, surely not?

Then, smack, another one, thrown with such force that it hit the sheet and smashed, she quickly turned in the direction that the eggs were coming from, the Harpers back garden and with her hands shielding the sun from her eyes she scanned the area, but could see nothing.

"What in heaven's name was going on?" Enid muttered under her breath, her suspicions starting to rise, she had a good idea that Stuart Harper, the little monkey, was behind this little escapade.

"Stuart Harper, is that you throwing those eggs? I can see you hiding behind the fence, show yourself now." She couldn't see him but thought she might be able to bluff him out of hiding.

Whizz, another egg hit the sheet with some force but not enough to break and it landed on the ground with a splat, so much for him showing himself. Then another was launched, and another.

"You little terror of a child, I'm coming round to your house to have words with your mother!" At this point Enid, who was absolutely fuming spun her ample frame round so as to exit the garden and go and give Mrs Harper a piece of her mind. Big mistake! A large double yolker cracked on the back of her hair and melted into her perm, her mouth fell open it total disbelief, "Why that little devil! Was he in for the high jump!"

But it wasn't over yet as one egg after another rained down on her, the target shifting from the sheets drying on the washing line to her floral day dress. She was under attack! And to make matters worse, she could hear the little sod laughing away to himself behind the fence. She turned, thrust herself forward, barging through the sheets she would have to wash all over again, flinging her arms out to clear them out of the way, head down, like a battering ram, towards that fence. And she had to hold her own here, as those eggs were coming thick and fast, and a fair few of them hitting their target, one of them hitting her chin and running between her ample heaving bosom.

Was she going to give him a piece of her mind, then she was going to drag him over that fence and round to his mam's house and give her a piece of her mind too, the terrible mother that she was. She pushed forward, towards that fence getting closer and closer, but wait a minute here, she stopped and took a moment to brush the egg from her face that had started to dribble into her eyes, was that two pair of hands full of eggs she could see? That little devil Stuart must have roped his brother Craig in as well, and Craig was usually such a good kid. This made Enid's heckles rise even further and she shoved the sleeves of her dress up her arms ready to grab the little devil that was Stuart Harper by the scruff of his scrawny neck. She leaned up against the fence with such force it creaked and groaned under the strain and then she stopped, dead, in her tracks, there he was Stuart Harper the little scallywag, but oh no! It couldn't be, her sweet little darling Erica stood at his side. Her youngest child, the apple of her and Lenny's eye, stood still in front of her, with hands full of eggs, poised to aim, caught in the act, covered in the corruption of the evil one that was Stuart Harper. Was that a glimpse of mischief in her lovely blue eyes or was it fear? Enid would never know and Erica must have done a good job to convince her of her innocence, as her punishment was never to play with him again, which on the odd occasion she ignored.

But I think I eventually worked it out, Erica told me that story loads of times. It started off with how he had made her do it but never with an explanation on what he said to convince her to. Her story was also very convincing at first, how she was in his evil grips and it was her covered in egg or the washing and she had made a democratic decision, so the washing it was. Enid, according to Erica, was never the intended target but after the first egg hit her there was no going back. There was a shift that happened the more times she told me, and her solemn tone was replaced with laughter and I began to wonder who was the bad influence on who? The more I listen to each and every retelling of that story the more I noticed that glimpse of mischief in her eyes. Stuart Harper played his last day as Erica's best friend on that warm balmy afternoon, and I was more than willing to step in to his shoes as Erica's new accomplice/apprentice/friend. A whole new chapter was about to begin and I was more than willing to immerse myself in it.

Nought to ten, the young years of my life all captured on paper. It's taken me quite some time to do and some nifty typing to get it all down. I'm sure there are loads of other stories if I dredged my brain that I could have documented but at last it's finished.

I hope that all of my family and friends who get a copy for their Christmas pressie from me, bother to take the time to read it. Who knows it may inspire you all to get your pencil and note pad out and have a go at doing it yourselves.

And there we have it….I know it's really bad grammar to start a sentence with and, but who cares it's my story.

And I've loved every minute of writing it.

15992118R00087

Printed in Great Britain
by Amazon